'It feels like only yesterday I was the youngest person in the room. I had my whole life in front of me. I had time to burn, I spent my whole day snogging boys, backcombing my hair and trying to dance like Pan's People. Now – it feels like two minutes later – I'm a little bit old. OK, I'm not in elasticated stockings or on Meals on Wheels or whizzing down the stairs on my stairlift but my life is more than half over. I've been there, done that, got the packamac. I'm so old that I remember dances with drum solos, the arrival of unisex hairdressers and I had a crush on Illya Kuryakin, which for people younger than me just looks like a bad Scrabble hand. What all this means is that I am grumpy. I have a bad hair life, my teenage daughter probably has a better sex life than I do, and if I skip plucking the beard for a couple of days, I have the start of some five o'clock shadow. Why wouldn't I be grumpy?'

Judith Holder is a prolific writer and television producer of many hours of peak-time Grumpy entertainment – in fact, you'd think she would be running out of grumps by now. Alas, there are many, many more where they came from. Judith co-wrote the hugely successful stage show *Grumpy Old Women Live* with her partner in crime Jenny Éclair, which has to date done two sell-out tours, a West End run and has taken Australia by storm. She lives so far north she sleeps in a duffel coat, has two teenage daughters, a husband who has to be reminded how to put a wash on, and a mother who needs running into town. How does she do it? Her hair looks rubbish, her bikini line needs waxing and she often forgets to bring her specs into work.

By Judith Holder

Grumpy Old Women
It's Not Grim Up North
The Secret Diary of a Grumpy Old Woman
Grumpy Old Holidays : The Official Handbook
Grumpy Old Couples

The Secret Diary of a

Grumpy Old Woman

AKA A Year in Big Knickers

JUDITH HOLDER

PHOENIX

A PHOENIX PAPERBACK

First published in Great Britain in 2006
by Weidenfeld & Nicolson
This paperback edition published in 2007
by Phoenix,
an imprint of Orion Books Ltd,
Orion House, 5 Upper St Martin's Lane,
London WC2H 9EA

An Hachette UK company

10 9 8 7 6

Text © Judith Holder 2006
Illustrations © Ruth Murray 2006

A CIP catalogue record for this book
is available from the British Library.

ISBN 978-0-7538-2128-2

Printed and bound in Great Britain by
CPI Mackays, Chatham ME5 8TD

The Orion Publishing Group's policy is to use papers
that are natural, renewable and recyclable products and
made from wood grown in sustainable forests. The logging
and manufacturing processes are expected to conform to
the environmental regulations of the country of origin.

www.orionbooks.co.uk

For mothers and their daughters everywhere

December

December 27th

Just when I thought I couldn't get any grumpier, that I was off the scale of grumpy, Christmas came along and made me grumpier than ever, which is saying something. As usual I worked myself up into a task-driven frenzy in an attempt to make it as perfect as Delia's, got into the annual panic about making sure that the lounge cushions were clean, the turkey was organic and Aunty Doreen got her Stilton by post on time. And boom – it's all over in a jiffy – and frankly with not that much to show for it except a house that looks like a bomb's hit it, Christmas tree needles (non-shed ones obviously) all over the hall, more clutter than I can hormonally tolerate and my mother-in-law still staying with us (6 days, 3 hrs and 12 mins and counting). The beds all need changing, the kitchen floor needs scrubbing, and the kitchen looks so bad Kim and Aggie might consider putting it on telly. I long to get all the cards off the mantelpiece and give the shelf a good clean, I long to get the Hoover into the corners behind the tree, long to get the tree

			WED	THU	FRI	SAT
3	4	5	*	*		
10	11	12	6	7	1	2
17	18	19	13	14	8	9
24	25	26	20	21	15	16
31	*	*	27	28	22	23
			*	29	(30)	

(mother-in-law goes home) YIPPEE!!

down and into
the skip; in short, I long to
get what my mother would call . . .
straight.

Thankfully, normality will soon be back. Trouble is Christmas occupied me for at least 100 hours, and that's a conservative estimate. That's the number of hours I reckon I spent on it. I haven't counted the July sales because I forgot which 'safe place' I decided to hide the Christmas presents . . . so it was utterly pointless. I haven't included making the Christmas cake because that was fun with ELDEST DAUGHTER. It made me feel like when she was at play school and we used to make cakes and have cuddles after lunch. I haven't included thinking time, time I would otherwise have spent thinking about something more constructive like work, or getting to the gym, which in my case means at all – and all this effort was for one day. And I daren't begin to think about how much money I spent . . . It's all exactly the same madness as last year and I'm an intelligent woman.

The telly was rubbish, I fell asleep in the Queen's Speech – in fact I think the Queen did too, it was so dull – and I lost the list of which relative gave what to which child, so yet again there will be the embarrassment of having to write thank you letters with the giveaway phrase, 'thank you for the Christmas gift' which means either you have written a standard letter to everyone, or you have forgotten what Uncle Fred gave you, or both. Other people seem to manage to have such organised lives in comparison.

Even the children have gone off Christmas. Now that the kids are teenagers I can spot their disenchantment, I can spot it because I remember my own disappointment, which started to set in the moment I discovered that Father Christmas was the biggest practical joke imaginable. In my case this was distressingly late – as an only child with no older siblings to tip you off you are rather vulnerable – and I was evidently impressionable: for several years I boasted that I saw the reindeer running around in Sutton Coldfield, 'saw them with my own eyes'. I was 12 when I discovered a piece of material in my mother's dressing-table drawer which was the same material as the crib cover for my baby doll and suddenly it all clicked into place – she, not Father Christmas and his elves, had made the crib. From that realisation the tables generally turn and you humour your parents because you think *they* find Christmas magical, when in fact *they* think *you* still do.

What's happened to my life since I got to be middle-aged? I seem to have more to do in any one day than I used to do in a whole month. But funnily enough at this exact time each year there is a little bit of calm, a little bit of peace and quiet when the festive season proper is over, and I can settle down to some serious lolling about in my dressing gown, and best of all lolling while filling in my brand-new diary, shiny and pristine in its bright red gorgeousness.

There's something about getting a new diary that reminds me of the first day of term at school. You wrote your name and class and timetable out in your neatest writing, planned your homework timetable, colour-coded your period due dates, underlined your birthday, or the boy you fancied's birthday, or Valentine's Day, and put a lot of exclamation marks round the anniversary of your

I love the Bay City Rollers

first snog. January was beautifully neat, but by the time you got into February it was scrawled with 'I love Noddy Holder' (or the Bay City Rollers), or notes and puzzling drawings from Jane Smith in Chemistry about what the missionary position means, or some spirobiro patterns you did when you were really really bored in Scripture. Which was most of the time. Thirty years or so on, the same will happen with my shiny new red diary – by February whatever system I adopt now of underlining my 'to do' lists, it'll have gone to pot – because my life is now one long long 'to do' list – it's called being a middle-aged woman, with a lot of errands to run, a saggy bottom and a need to tidy the airing cupboard.

I fill in all the bits at the front, well OK not the blood group bits – I'm not an anorak – and I put the family birthdays in, I put all my special encrypted codes to remember my pin numbers and passwords – cunningly clever charts of numbers with circled bits and crossings out that look like the Enigma code and look accidental but are brilliantly intentional, because remembering them all in my head is now a scientific impossibility since my memory banks are full – one new code, such as a new door code at work, goes in and something has to go out – like my mother's birthday or the next date to worm the dog. There is only so much of this stupid information a woman can retain. The encrypted codes I make up seem like the simplest thing to remember when I invent them – like the year I had my first pet hamster or the ballet school I went to in Weston-super-Mare or the year my father was born minus 10 . . . they all seem so fantastically easy to remember, until the

HOW TO REMEMBER MY PIN

$$\frac{2}{1} \times \frac{b}{2c} = e^3$$

time comes when I have to remember them and then I forget or I
forget where I wrote down the secret code. Last year I was
foolish enough to make one or two new codes up, keep the
potential identity thieves on their toes . . . Naturally I instantly
forgot how I had decided to remember it all, and so there were
tears and sick on the pavement at a cashpoint when the machine
swallowed my card . . . and even more tears and sick when I
tried to get the bank to believe it was me trying to get a new card
not someone else pretending to be me. Makes me feel hot and
angry just thinking about it.

I can do all this diary filling in now because of this little gap
of relative calm, of relative inertia, with some proper slobbing
about in my slippers and dressing gown, after the hell that was
Christmas, and before we all get back into the school run and
the nine to five. It's the time when I convince myself that next
year is going to be infinitely more organised, infinitely more
serene, sunnier and generally sorted than the one just gone. I
really am going to go jogging, going to use the public library
more, I'm going to delegate more jobs around the house and not
let work get to me, especially my boss, Jocasta.

I'm ashamed to admit that even the Christmas presents given to me were the usual disappointment – not quite the jumper I had in mind, not quite the right perfume and not quite the right book – which makes the whole thing feel even more futile and

maddeningly stupid. As usual the present that was the most disappointing was the one from the GRUMPY OLD MAN – not because he hasn't made an effort, not because he hasn't tried to please, but because deep down I always hope he will buy me a stunning diamond, a fabulous necklace or an absurdly romantic piece of jewellery with a little note in it telling me how completely gorgeous and irresistible I am, which clearly would be fibbing, but would make me feel like number one top sex kitten. This year he bought me a bright neon green padded outdoor coat – which is about as far away from a romantic diamond or jewellery gift as you can get – but he cannot be held responsible for this badly judged present since, guess what – I chose it myself, circled it in the catalogue and put it on his side of the bed. As outdoor coats go it is spot on – dreamy toasty warm for walking the dog or going to the market, although flattering it is not. In fact it makes me look like a lagged boiler and is such a bright green it is no doubt visible from outer space . . . Which means it would be very handy in an emergency. I could wave the helicopter down. Save the day. But it's emphatically not sexy, so despite the fact that I asked for it for Christmas, I am starting to blame him – which is ridiculously unfair. That's the kind of person I am to live with. Full of contradictions. You'd think by my age I'd have got myself a bit more sorted, but I feel a little like my daughters, a bit like a teenager, a bit pulled in different directions – do I still want to be a little bit sexy, a little bit minxy, or am I ready to get into a round of golf and a life of table-top sales at the WI and be done with it? I don't know.

Dodgiest present was a cut-glass decanter (are there any other sort?) that had been taken out of its box and rewrapped. You can tell that because it's lost its little sticky label and anyway what would anyone sensible do with a decanter except wrap it up, hope you kept the presentation box and send it to someone else? If you're really smart and you have the time you can find out where they sell them and try to change them for credit vouchers. That would be a triumph. A sort of punching-the-air-type triumph. But that would require a great deal of time and effort so have done the next best thing . . . have put in my 'recycled present' cupboard.

As a family, we've all had an overdose of quality time with one another, played charades and Monopoly and Knock-out Whist until we can no more, and now Boxing Day is over the bets are off, and we all spend the day in our own rooms, on our beds, reading the paper or MSN messaging our friends. Well, we would do except the mother-in-law doesn't seem to have booked a train ticket till Saturday. Which is a worry.

She's everywhere. I come down in the morning and she's already in the kitchen, dressed, lipstick on, hair done, wanting to talk. She makes me feel lazy and a bit common, as my mother would say, slobbing around still in my dressing gown at 7.30. Normally I like the hour before everyone gets up, I get myself into a bit of pottering about, but when someone's talking non-stop to you, like she does, it proves impossible. She asks 'Can I do anything to help?' in the way guests do – without actually doing anything at all – and starts asking

Put back money into YOUNGEST'S piggy bank !!

endless questions about the OLD MAN, her beloved only son, about ELDEST DAUGHTER – what have we done about her student loan? Is she taking her laptop away with her and if so is it on the household insurance? – and about YOUNGEST DAUGHTER – have I checked whether the sub-aqua teacher at the pool is CRB cleared? Am I sure that she is not already into boys? Shouldn't I be forbidding her to go out without tights? I listen, but after 18 years of marriage frankly there's not the attention to detail on my part that there was.

She frightened me to death when I was still just 'the girlfriend', when I was on my best behaviour, dressing to impress and making out I was going to be her new best friend. Now I'm counting the days until Saturday, and we can all stop using the teapot and a tablecloth for supper. The moment she's gone we'll

To DO
Get boiler serviced
Ring Aunt Dorothy to thank for presents
Fill in Tax-form
SAVE MONEY!
Write 'taking back' list
Bunion plasters
Check sub-aqua teacher CRB cleared
Find out what CRB cleared means
Ring station about train times
Find receipts for taking back presents
Bin liners

be eating in front of the telly, out of tins probably, in an involuntary and unspoken act of rebellion. Can't wait.

December 28th

It feels like only yesterday I was the youngest person in the room, I had my whole life in front of me, I had time to burn, I spent my whole day snogging boys and backcombing my hair. I was a young thing, with a lovely body, life was fun, and I hadn't a care in the world, and now – it feels like two minutes later – I'm a little bit old. OK I'm not in elasticated stockings or on Meals on Wheels or whizzing down the stairs on my stairlift, but my life is more than half over.

I've been there, done that, got the packamac, I'm so old that I remember dances with drum solos, the arrival of unisex hairdressers and had a crush on Illya Kuryakin. Which if you're too young and you don't remember *The Man from U.N.C.L.E.* just looks like a bad Scrabble hand. Never mind over the hill, I am over the other side and nearly down at the bottom. And the view is slightly different. What all this adds up to is that I am grumpy. For a start I have a bad hair life, my teenager daughter has a better sex life than I do, and skip plucking the beard for a couple of days and I have the start of some five o' clock shadow. So why wouldn't I be grumpy?

I'm allowed to be grumpy, I've earned it . . . I lived through Boney M and Bucks Fizz, leg warmers and the Crossroads Motel, I deserve to be grumpy. And as your self-appointed form captain, I think I can safely say that we all feel that none of this is our fault. Left to our own devices we are naturally peachy,

change mophead

cheery people, but everything and everyone else lets us down. It's a day-in day-out sort of thing. Being full-on grumpy is a full-time job. Sometimes I wonder how I have time to go to work.

December 30th

The first credit card bill arrives with Christmas shopping transactions on. It is so bad I think there must be a mistake, someone must be shopping on my card, because something has gone hideously wrong. Of course something has gone hideously wrong, I have spent too much money. Again. So the taking back routine has to begin because, whether I like it or not, I have to try to claw back some money. Hence I throw myself into taking things back and since no one else bothered to keep the receipts, the whole wretched experience is going to be very, very annoying indeed.

Shopping makes me very grumpy indeed. People assume that women love shopping, but no woman I know does. These days when I am shopping I am so grumpy I feel drawn to using a stick. It would be useful for everyday life, to flick people with who are annoying me, holding me up, dawdling, knocking into me, getting in the queue before me. Maybe a little cane, or one of those rambler's poles, something to flick at people's ankles, stop them putting their feet up on train seats, stopping them leaving their rubbish or spitting on the pavement. There would be a hundred and one uses. Or I'd like one of those huge clompy prams young mothers have now, with huge wheels and chassis the size of a small car. I could accidentally on purpose snag people's ankles with it,

CALL
WINDOW
CLEANER

or use it as a ram raider on young people who are throwing litter on the ground or being objectionable. Except if I did have such a pram I would look like a mad old bat who should be in a mental institution or a tramp, since there would be no baby in it.

Other people are becoming a serious source of grump for me. Shopping would be fine if there were no other people involved. I'd like my own little pedestrian lane, my own check-out queue, I might even share it with other nice grumpy old women, and my own parking bays. Because we are in a hurry, we are hormonally challenged and our lives are made up of dreary little jobs no one else can be bothered to do.

I start the taking-back task and plot a time-efficient route round the city centre. At least the Christmas shoppers won't be there; I'll be able to park on the top floor of the multi-storey, just nip straight into the big stores, be home in time to have a sit-down and watch an episode of *Desperate Housewives* . . . But it's strangely busy on the way into town. Actually, nearly as busy as it was the week before Christmas. Why? How could I have forgotten? The sales have started. That is just so very cruel. You get the Christmas shopping out of the way, you go in to take it all back and you get the crowds and the hassle and the queues all over again. Except this time there is an additional queue at Exchanges and Refunds. A queue so long that they rope it off like at Disney. They obviously staff it with the newest, youngest of their assistants; better still, they stick up a sign saying PLEASE BEAR WITH US, STAFF TRAINING IN PROGRESS, which means that every single pair of knickers, every single travel clock that is being taken back because it was loathed and detested by its recipient is having to be cross-referenced on a big long list.

Because they've reduced it now. And if you don't have the receipt, your nice friend who queued up to buy it in the first place paid £29.99 for it and they are offering you £10.99 for it, in vouchers, not even in real cash. Which all takes about half an hour per customer, so you give up, or you run out of time, and you could simply run up and down in the shop and scream and scream and scream until you're sick. Or you could run amok among ladies separates and throw everything on the floor so they have to pick it all up again. You give up and lug some of it back home, which is a low point, especially knowing it is not even nice enough to go into the recycled-presents cupboard.

UNCLE MAX??

SOFS

mad woman at no 45 when she gives me something??

for tombola?

To DO
Fill in tax form
Shave underarms
Sheer black tights (extra large)
Book chiropodist
Find replacement mop head
Ring Warburtons about New Year's Eve
Use public library more

December 31st

As a teenager New Year's Eve was the bit of Christmas that you looked forward to the most. You'd been imprisoned with family for what seemed like an eternity, pretended to like vile novelty socks given to you, and received more bath bubbles and notelets with blackberries and squirrels on them than anyone could hope to use in an entire year. You deserved to be able to break out on your own a little bit, let your hair down and go a bit wild. As a child I occasionally watched my parents get a little bit wild on New Year's Eve. When I say wild I mean they'd do the Twist to Chubby Checker. I saw them kiss one year, no, snog even, which was frighteningly shocking. The thing about being an only child is that you can persuade yourself that your parents only did it once, OK maybe twice, and in fact you do persuade yourself of this, that their sex life was entirely functional, entirely minimal. But the snog seemed to imply something different. It was a relief when someone turned the telly on and put a stop to it.

Now as I watch my own ELDEST DAUGHTER get ready for New Year's Eve, I realise – as realise I must – that she is about to start her own life, that in seven months' time she will have effectively gone, on her gap-year trip to Ghana, and then on to university. My nest is emptying. My stomach flips. I feel sick at the thought. She goes out, naturally, with a summer dress on, no coat, no tights and sling-back shoes, and looking simply gorgeous. How could any boy appreciate her? How could they ever know how special she is? How can anyone love her as much as I do? At her age, at New Year's Eve parties I was probably snogging someone under a pile of donkey jackets in the spare room, so logic tells me she will be doing something remarkably similar. Which is something else to worry about, not least

because she is staying the night at
Laura's which if I was doing an
impression of her I'd say with some
mimed inverted commas, because
staying at Laura's I imagine is code for
'don't even think about coming to
collect me, I can do what I like now . . .
and if I choose to stay out till 3am frankly you can't stop me'.

CALL WINDOW CLEANER

    I get wistful and nostalgic, think about how my life has changed
over the years and how what I do on New Year's Eve has changed
with it. In my twenties I went away with friends at New Year.
Rented cottages by the sea, with far fewer bedrooms than couples,
slept in until two in the afternoon, drank bottles of red wine, got
silly and giggly, stayed up all night . . . played drunken games of
sardines. I called my parents at 12 and talked to them pityingly.
I wore tight jeans, I looked good, I talked a lot. Smoked a lot.
Flirted a lot. I had a ball. Then in my thirties New Year's Eve was
an occasion to chum up with close friends with small children.
Staying at each other's houses with a car full of Babygros and
changing bags and listening devices and everyone pale and dizzy
with exhaustion. Dancing with a baby on your shoulder to West
End Girls, bouncing baby on the bed with you in the morning.
Snuggling up to them. Smelling their hair, bathing them and
blowing bubbles through the flannel, singing 'Me and My Teddy
Bear', drying them after bath time on your lap in a warm towel
with a hood on it, reading some Ahlberg *Peepo* or *Bye Bye Baby*.
In reality I was too exhausted to appreciate it, but of course
looking back now that ELDEST's days at home are literally
numbered, it seems in retrospect a golden time. Even something
as awful as taking it in turns to do the early shift with baby
(meaning post-4am) seems memorably wonderful. Reason tells
me that my memory has played tricks on me, but it's still hard.

And now I'm a Grumpy Old Woman, New Year's Eve feels like just another evening, the magic has gone, all that false and alcohol-induced revelry simply makes me want to reach for a hot-water bottle and a good book. But you can't. It is not allowed just to have a nice early night and a good night's sleep. My mother calls. She's in Devon with a friend. It is her first New Year's Eve without my father. And she sounds surprisingly well.

We go to the Warburtons' drinks party. I find the small talk overwhelmingly dull until someone tells me the Foresters have split up. It's always the couples you think are blissfully happy that split up. It's like the curse of *Hello!* magazine, the moment they do a feature about how much they love one another, or redo their vows or whatever it is celebrities endlessly do, you know it's doomed . . . they'll be divorced by the end of the year.

At the party, YOUNGEST DAUGHTER hangs out with all the other young people playing pool, and I am a little envious. Envious that they're having more fun, have some loud music on and there is a lot of giggling, whereas with the grown-ups there are a lot of dull groups of people talking about their 'nice quiet family Christmas' and their loft lagging, garden features and skiing holidays. Dull dull dull dull. Trouble is at my age you can't take the edge off it all . . . you can't drink too much (you're driving) and you don't take drugs, so you get bored very quickly. Or I do. I am trapped in a body that people think means I am dull. Look 20 or 30 and people assume you're fascinating, even though you're not, but get to my age, get a bit of life behind you and frankly something interesting to say, and young people assume you are a non-person. You could tell them something really outrageous, like pretend you once used your Rampant Rabbit to make a meringue, really startle them, and they'd still just look through you. I can't be bothered, I feel wasted on them. I wander into the teenagers' room, which I feel is my spiritual home, in the hope that they will take me in, assimilate me as an honorary adolescent, which is what I feel like, and ask me to stay. They don't. Actually YOUNGEST asks me to go away.

Lost and feeling I don't fit anywhere I open the back door for some fresh air, wanting to go home, and find a group of smokers, standing out in the freezing cold, with a bottle of red wine and some malt whisky. They are pretty drunk, and they assume I've sneaked outside for a ciggie too. There is a lovely camaraderie that happens with smokers now that they are despised and told to stand outside; they bond and become the naughty smokers, feel a bit wicked and behave like overgrown teenagers. Sometimes I find this irritating, but tonight I actually find them fun. I find myself having a cigarette for the first time in 15 years, and a very large glass of red wine. Talk gets on to sex and there is a lot of giggling. Tall flicky-haired girl says her friend is in terrible relationship – sex happens twice a week – I sympathise, feel a bit dizzy, a bit hazy round the edges, say, 'God, how awful, I can only manage once a week and sometimes that's a bit of an effort.' Soon realised flicky-haired woman and the others means twice a week is appallingly infrequent. Felt stupid and took hasty retreat back inside but not before I had had two cigarettes and about three glasses of red wine, a beaker full of malt whisky – and this on top of the white wine I had already consumed when bored out of my brain earlier.

Text ELDEST DAUGHTER 'Happy New Year, love you loads' and send it, then realise I sent it to someone at work – must put my glasses on when I text in future.

Had a nice dance to 'Ili Ilo Silver Lining' with the GRUMPY OLD MAN, caught YOUNGEST watching horrified at the old man's Mick Jagger impression and my evident lack of embarrassment at anything. Spared her the sight of us kissing, knowing the damage done by my own equivalent.

Stagger out of party and YOUNGEST tells me off like I am naughty teenager and she is huffy mother: 'You're drunk, have you been smoking, God it's disgusting. And at your age . . .'

Got taxi home and driver looked strangely unfamiliar – he'd picked us up loads of times before but looked different. I asked him what had happened? He said he'd shaved off his moustache, apparently everyone keeps telling him he looks ten years younger. If only shaving mine off would have the same effect.

By the time I follow the old man to bed I can hear him snoring from the landing already. So much for life beginning at 40.

TO DO
Book optician for new glasses
Bottle bank
Tax return urgent
Change beds
Mend broken zip on brown skirt
Facial hair wax kit
Tweezers
Strepsils

NEW YEARS EVE'S RESOLUTIONS

I will NOT eat biscuits at work

I will be more positive

I will exercise more

I will relax more

I will be more informed about the news

I will be nicer to my mother in law

I will have more alcohol days — at least two a week

I will live for TODAY (at weekends)

January

New Year's Day

Woke up and felt perfectly OK, got downstairs, put the kettle on, let the cat in and the dog out, and congratulated myself on being able to take my drink nearly as well as when I was in my twenties, instead of being incapacitated with one glass as of late. Then suddenly and without any warning the hangover kicked in, felt like I had walked into a plate-glass window.
It was then I noticed some of the things that I had done the night before on coming home, some of the tell-tale signs that mean that yes, I was indeed extremely drunk. In my attempt to convince myself that I was absolutely fine and in control I had laid the table up for breakfast complete with cereal bowls, spoons, serviettes and milk jug (something I would never do sober) and had tried to put the cereal packets on the table but scooped up just about everything in the cupboard, flour, risotto rice, couscous, lentils and topped it off with scary bucket and mop arrangement like a drunken youth would put a traffic cone on a statue.

Crawl upstairs and find more evidence of very drunk behaviour, shoes taken off and placed neatly by wardrobe, mobile on charge (but on wrong charger), and Vaseline Intensive Care smeared all over carpet and bathroom floor after major feet moisturising attempts – it's a miracle I didn't fall and crack my head open on the bath... all of it signs of me trying to persuade myself that I am not only in control but very very sober indeed, but a drunken 'to do' list written out for tomorrow in big scrawly writing barely legible – saying 'chill out more' – final and clinching evidence of total drunken brain type thoughts. Scary.

Have to spend entire day in bed, as not able to cope with sudden neck or head movements. What sort of a mother role model am I turning into?

Weight Watchers are sending me irritating emails every day presumably because I once went on to the website and they know at this time of year it's hard to find an excuse not to try to lose weight. They've been saving it up and now have a whole special sales force targeting the greedy en masse, getting them to sign up for their classes. Because they know at this time of the year you are vulnerable, and – face it – you've eaten so much over Christmas you hardly came up for air. Of course worrying about my weight is nothing new, not something that has plagued me just since I hit middle age. I only wish that I had appreciated my lovely upper arms before they turned into the dreaded bat wings, wish I hadn't worried about my thighs so much because – hey – that was nothing compared to the stuff that's happened lately – the midriff bulge has now hit big time. I'm getting fat all over, fat stomach, fat arms, fat neck, fat chin, I look sort of beefy, bigger all round; sometimes I think my head's getting smaller so that if I wore a floral summer dress and some high heels with American Tan tights, I'd look like a transvestite, like Dame Edna or Dick Emery.  Young male colleagues at work, I notice, seem a bit reluctant to be alone with me, avoid eye contact if we are in the lift or in the stationery room alone – maybe they think I'm going to pounce.

It's a tough one to accept that your powers of sexual attraction are frankly dwindling, and that the men who do look at you now are slightly better looking than John McCririck. It's all so hard when evidently in my thirties I was so gorgeous, I really was – I've seen photos – although tragically at the time it didn't seem so. I could manipulate men with my sex appeal. I mean I wasn't some sort of mad sex pervert, but if I wanted to get a man to do something for me I could generally turn it on and get my way. Now if I did get off with a bloke younger than me or very good-looking indeed the dynamics would have changed fundamentally: they'd assume I was grateful rather than the other way round. But it's taken me ages to realise something totally obvious. Somehow I always told myself that being attractive to the opposite sex had nothing to do with your looks, men fell for women who made them laugh, interested them, that they like . . . fell for women in particular with personality, vivacity and humour. I always rather pitied girls who were dumb blondes, good-looking but either indifferently clever or indifferently interesting. Until now. Suddenly I have woken up to the fact that men, old and young, fat and thin, tall and short, like women who look good. They like women who look good more than they like women who make them laugh, or are one of the lads, or buy a round of drinks, or can kick a tyre or work a Black and Decker, and now my life seems to have been a bit of a wasteland sexually. How could I have got this so wrong? And what seems so unfair is that it works for men the other way: all the polls say that women find men attractive who make them laugh, who have an engaging personality . . . nothing to do with their looks.

It doesn't stop me wanting to be more attractive to men, even though I am frighteningly middle-aged, so like everyone else I am endlessly trying to lose weight. I do want to be skinnier, but I also want to eat Kettle chips and have a glass of wine once the dishwasher's on and the day is done. Because life for a grumpy old woman is – let's face it – more exhausting than pulling along a juggernaut with a rope round your waist. Result . . . The middle-age spread is settling in.

To Do
Low-fat spread
Look into food allergist
Facial exerciser thing
Corn plasters
Buy soya milk (low-fat)

January 3rd

What is it with me and personal admin? I am incapable of doing it. The bank statements come and I put them in a safe place, the credit card bills come and I put them somewhere prominent to remind me to pay them, and then they all promptly and spitefully disappear. I really think I should be excused it all. I have enough to do already – can't the police do it for us, or our grumpy old men? I think grumpy old women, without whom no kitchen bin would be emptied, no bed would be changed and no towel folded, should be exempt.

It's not just the stuff from the bank and the insurance company, it's all the dreary but time-consuming things that come home from school, endless forms and letters with bits to tear off at the bottom, and Miss wants £6.50 in a named envelope in cash by tomorrow, and a packed lunch without nuts sent on Friday week along with a full Elizabethan costume
for the

Dear Mrs Rowbottom
I am really sorry that I lost your
...iginal letter regarding my
...t daughter's history
...nonth. Thi...

Macbeth production and a donation for the spring fair. Can't they run the school themselves? Some days I think they might as well give me a desk in the staff room.

FIND PLUMBER

The whole personal admin nightmare is at its worst this time of year, more or less precisely this time of year. You've been too busy doing secret Santas and making chestnut stuffing to do anything other than chuck bank statements, visa statements, direct-debit forms in a big pile on the dressing table for the last six weeks. Bad enough. Then those stupid ads come on the telly telling you cheerily how easy it is to do your tax form on-line . . . and you can ignore it no longer. The tax form has to be done. Which is to personal admin what root-canal work is to a scale and polish. This wretched form has to be done. Now. Dozens of maddening pieces of paper and numbers and spreadsheets have to be found. Like the annual scramble to find the form the building society sent you with your interest details from your savings account has self-destructed and disappeared, along with all the rest of the documents that it is going to take you days to find or replace, like your P45 or whatever they call it now, and your endowment policy. The whole thing is beyond tedious.

I get on the phone to the building society and, guess what, I am in a queue, with dozens of stalling tactics and holding patterns. The first one is fill in your account details and your sort codes and so on, and then your password and then you get to another menu, and another and another, and then when you do get through to someone they ask it you all over again. Truth is the whole nation is ringing up for a copy of their interest statements. And, guess what, they charge you £20 for the duplicate. Next year I am going to do it early.

To Do

Put notes to self in diary to ensure
*   early completion of tax form*
Renew RAC membership
Organise charity shop STINT for youngest
*   to do her Duke of Edin Award*
Take shoes to repairers
Find receipt for unwanted trainers
Batteries

January 6th

   Back to work. Obviously work is meant to be annoying, but going back after a two-week break is enough to make even the non-grumpy very grumpy indeed. Back to the world where everyone talks in a silly office language; when you have been away from it for a week or two, you notice it even more. Everyone's talking about initiatives that 'innovate change', or how to do '360-degree feedback', or how to 'manage delegation' or, my favourite, 'noisy ideas'. The older I get the more infuriating I find the whole thing, everyone talks about 'levelling playing fields' and 'bringing things to the table' (or, worse, 'to the party'), or 'synergy' or 'blue sky thinking'. You can't just have a good idea, you have to 'think outside the box', or 'push the envelope' or 'run it up a flagpole'. What a load of old tosh! I heard someone today answer the phone and say that Robin had just 'stepped out of the office' like he'd just dared to put one foot out of the door into the corridor and then rushed back again. What's wrong with just saying he's gone out? Robin and Jocasta (my she-who-must-be-obeyed boss) are having a bit of a thing, everyone thinks. He does a lot of simpering and laughing very loudly at her (not very funny) jokes and says she looks lovely when she so does not. When we were away at conference there was a lot of ridiculous talk at breakfast from them both about their 'individual' rooms. Gosh does yours overlook the car park, oh mine's really rather nice, etc. Obviously to try to put us all off the scent. Just makes it all the more obvious in my view.

Bloke I sent text to on New Year's Eve looks sceptical when I tell him I sent it to him by mistake, like it took some drink to tell him I loved him loads and fancied the pants off him, and then I sobered up and lost my nerve. Wouldn't mind but he is rather good-looking and no doubt will have emailed his young colleagues that I am scary menopausal woman on the sexual warpath.

The sheer hard work of being back in the office is a shock. A relentless non-stop round of emails, texts and messages. You can't even get away from it all at home. In the old days you just had the answer machine to check when you got home, now you have the email and the voice mail on the mobile and the answer machine in the kitchen. There is simply no respite at all. And what is it with people and their mobiles? They have to be on them or pretending to be on them at all times, look busy, everyone has to look busy, all the time. Not to look busy would be a crime. Seeing someone with the Blue tooth thing walking along apparently talking to themselves, I mean we will all have them surgically implanted in our brains soon, got to happen . . . I'm so old I remember public call boxes. Haven't seen one in use for years. At least you could pretend the queue was too long if you didn't want to talk to anyone. These days everyone can be contacted at all times, on the bus, in the loo, everywhere. People are starting to have two mobiles I notice, presumably one for work that they get paid for by the company, and one for social. Or as someone put it the other day, one for work and one for sex. I think I know which of mine would ring the most.

And all the so-called time-saving devices that are so not saving you time, have to be charged, the laptop, the iPod, the whole house is a mass of cables and rechargers and batteries, all of them needing more attention than a naughty toddler. All of them have different chargers and attachments you might know – more things to lose, or change or replace.

And of course you lug so much around, by the time you've got your laptop, your mobile, your cables and your personal organiser, you are well and truly weighed down. Might as well just plug yourself into the mains and be done with it.

One of the occupational hazards of being of a certain age is that your boss will inevitably be younger and probably sillier than you are. Which is true in my case. Jocasta has her own glass-walled office, and wears silly impractical high heels, some absurdly low-cut tops, and does a lot of showing off. Not sure what it is she actually does all day in terms of work, as most of it seems to get delegated down – she's one of the new breed of women who is married to a house husband, and since they have no kids I assume she returns home to stunning clean house, candlelit dinner and a lot of 'me' time, which means she doesn't have any of the millions of other things to think about that I do; she can concentrate on booking her manicurist, or her life coach or her weekend in Italy. People ask me how I manage to fit everything in with two kids and a full-time job and I say I manage it because my bikini line needs waxing, my hair looks a mess and the ironing needs doing. Jocasta has no such problems.

TO DO
Book bikini-line wax
Buy new smart top - striped? - for work
Cat food and litter
Send in tombola stuff
Dental tape
Take picture frame back to <u>Ikea</u>
                    — wrong size for poster
Measure poster

January 8th

    Saw gorgeous recipe for polenta with red peppers, mixed it and rolled it and honestly couldn't see the difference between it and wallpaper paste. Bloody Domestic Goddesses.

TO DO
Buy pan scourers
Use library more

Polenta garnish

Metric/Imperial	lettuce leaf
1	medium-sized to...
½	Polenta
250g	egg mayonna...
1 tbs	tomato pu...
¼ tsp	lemon j...
4 or 5 drops	sugar
3 or 4 pinches	

January 10th

ELDEST announces that she will no longer be coming on family holidays with us. Am distraught. Go to Lunn Poly and gather up all the most expensive long-haul brochures and put them on her bed. Later drop in and say, 'Is there anything that takes your fancy, darling?' Which is tantamount to saying 'OK, anything, we'll do anything, we'll spend anything to get you to come with us, for us to try and extend your childhood in any way at all'. She looks interested. I feel a sense of relief, then she says she might be interested but would want to bring boyfriend. What boyfriend?

TO DO

Get fit (try jogging?)
Talk to ELDEST about contraception
Book romantic weekend for GRUMPY
                    OLD MAN and me
Ring my mother about marmalade recipe
Buy more pan scourers

January 12th

Boyfriend coming to Sunday lunch. Must mean she has been seeing boyfriend for weeks, months, or, God forbid, is pregnant by him, since the Sunday-lunch slot is to meeting the parents what the Saturday-night slot is to dating. GRUMPY OLD MAN and I don't say anything to one another, but clearly we are both making more of an effort than usual. He's not in his old gardening jeans and I put some lipstick and a skirt on. I get the nice china out, since if he turns out to be major catch as in his father is hugely wealthy property developer or Sir Macalpine or Mr Tesco's then obviously he will need to be persuaded that ELDEST will turn into sophisticated, slim and still gorgeous middle-aged domestic goddess. Since he will be looking at me to establish above, this is a worry . . . in fact it is not really going to be possible given the scale of the problem, but I plan on being very very amusing, very very young at heart.

Tragically forgot to take drying washing down off rack over Aga and a pair of my very large knickers was perilously close to brushing the top of his hair as he came in. He is taller than any of us, and while making gravy in kitchen alone I quickly swapped them with a pair of ELDEST's teeny-weeny ones, so he thinks he might be marrying into a family of sex minxes who stay that way well into middle age. I liked him. GRUMPY OLD

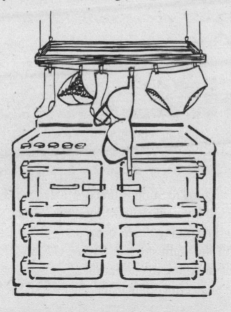

MAN asked him where he lives in great detail, and what his parents do, not exactly subtle I thought, but I listened very carefully to the answers. He wants to go into textiles. I pretended I knew what that meant, but these days being a plumber is so lucrative that it's as good as being a banker, but with less hassle – so you don't really know where you are. How old and middle-aged do I sound?

To Do
Go Jogging
Buy smaller pants
Google textile jobs
Buy new non-stick pan

January 15th

Jocasta calls stupid 'interface' meeting at 5pm. She has nothing else to do obviously . . . So I come home from work late to find place a tip, the girls eating out of ice-cream tubs, watching completely banal programme called *America's Next Top Model*, and I do my usual lecture about the fact that they should be watching *Planet Earth* or a landmark History series. They give me that look which means 'you sad old cow get a life'. They're forever glued to hideous programmes with Paris Hilton, or gay fashion designers in LA or shocking rubbish about the latest anal-bleaching craze. It has to be stopped. I decide to take immediate action, so off I skip upstairs to cancel the satellite subscription, knowing that a rota or house rule will be impossible to police; time it right and get the cancellation done now and the TV might even go black in the middle of *America's Top Model*. Which would be a triumph. Get on the phone queue, first option is are you an existing customer or a new customer, I know that the new customer is going to get through in a nanosecond and existing customers are going to be in a holding pattern for 20 minutes, so I try to buck the system and pretend I am a new customer and want a new or additional satellite dish. I tried this and they just put me back to the start of the queue again so nothing gained at all. Am deflated. Will sort tomorrow.

Only been back at work for a few days after Christmas 'break' and already I get to 9.30pm and I am desperate to sit down with a glass of wine. No, really need to sit down. By the time I have got my bags by the door for the next morning, sorted packed lunches out for the girls, got chops out of the freezer and ironed three shirts, having done a day's work work, I am officially bad-tempered. What I want to do now is loll on the sofa and chill out. What I don't want to do is chat on the phone.

Which is why when the phone rings and it's a cold caller selling me some double glazing that's bad, but not as bad as a friend calling up for a chat. 'Are you all right to chat?' they say. No I'm not, but do I say that? No . . . 'How are you anyway?' I say. 'How's it all going?' My heart sinks. It's not that I don't love my friends, but I have been on the phone all day, on the go all day, and frankly I just want to keep it brief – to something like 'see you Friday, 6.30, and what does Keith want for his birthday?' That's it. And then a nice glass of wine and a real chat when we meet. Worst thing is if you ring someone and hope to get the answer machine, pre-empt the chat . . . call during the day, and they're at home having a day off and have even more time to chat than normal. Answer machines are glorious for talk avoidance. But texting even more glorious.

TO DO
Cancel Satellite subscription
Ring Anne to fix up girly lunch
Go jogging
Email Suzanne
Screen wash
Is car MOT still valid? — rattle
Service boiler   in car

January 18th

Was planning on jogging but pavement
looked icy.
Worried about having a fall. Because at
my age I wouldn't fall over, I would have
a fall and for some reason that's much
more serious.

GO JOGGING
(tomorrow)

January 19th

Jog for 15 minutes. Have to stop at lamp-posts for panting.
Am so bad at running, never mind jogging, I look just like I am in
a bit of a hurry. Need to get home to-let-the-electrician-in-sort-
of-run . . . Will have to forget jogging. Might try swimming in
lunch hours instead.

Get back on the cancelling satellite TV case – and get through
to a woman who interrogates me as to why I am cancelling, which
seems both pointless and impertinent. Takes a good 20 minutes

and I still have to tell the bank to cancel the direct debit. Which will take another 40 minutes.

Come downstairs in a triumph and tell girls that I have done something with their best interests at heart – cancelled satellite as of now. YOUNGEST bursts into tears, says she will be a nothing, a nonentity at school if she can't watch *The Simpsons* and *My Big Fat Obnoxious Boss*. ELDEST says she was going to use the History channel for revision, which was her trump card. So yours truly feels an utter noo na and has to reverse whole thing. Triumph and moral high ground completely backfired. I am back on the satellite TV customer services (so-called) menu, this time have to key in new customer, which I thought would get me to the top of the queue and sure enough they answer within five minutes, but as I am renewing an old subscription I need to call another number and I have to cancel the direct debit before they will fill out a new membership. If I had a cricket bat I would lob it into the screen and smash it.

To DO —
Find out how eBay works
Go to library to loan educationally
        sound videos for girls
Buy magic swimming costume with
    pull-in elasticated front like in
            GOOD HOUSEKEEPING mag

CALL
WINDOW
CLEANER

January 26th

    Burns Night. And the post-Christmas corporate hospitality machine gets going. I go because I feel I should. The evening always starts with such promise. You know you should be enjoying it, everyone else does seem to be enjoying it. You feel a freak. You're trapped in the seating plan from hell, sitting for three hours next to someone who bores you almost literally to death. They tell you in minute detail about their job because they are big in cardboard packaging, tell you so much about their dreary lives you know about the sandwich fillings that they take in on Mondays, Tuesdays and Fridays and on Thursdays in leap years, they talk about themselves non-stop until you think there is nothing else to tell you and then they tell you about the sandwich filling they are having tomorrow. More depressing even than that, they say they are going to tell you a really funny story. Yes, well I'll be the judge of that. My heart sinks when someone tells me that. I know it's not going to be funny, think I am turning into a miserable old cow.

TO DO

Book holiday

Loo Rolls

Find out about eBay

Call school re maths module

January 29th

Am officially suffering from SAD syndrome, spend all my waking hours in darkness, and am so cold at night I am sleeping in my fleece and track-suit bottoms. It's called living up north. Look pasty, feel fat and forty . . . . Maddeningly the OLD MAN is wearing better than I am; his grey hair is looking a bit distinguished, he looks good in his suit for work. Stare at myself in bathroom mirror, flip over to shaving side that magnifies . . . dreadful shock. I have the start of some six o'clock shadow. Could do with shaving every other day. Feel overwhelmingly fed up about state of neck, chin and face. Do something really mad. Spot YOUNGEST's purple hair dye – the one she got from the hippy shop in town – in cabinet and go for it. Paste it on and hey presto, now I have purple streaks in my hair. I think it says something very definite about me . . . Says I may be pushing 50 but I'm still fun, still cool, still in the land of the living.

ELDEST sees my hair and says that she will never ever be able to bring anyone home again.

RING HAIRDRESSER

January 30th

See first Easter eggs in the shops. Could kill.

February

February 5th

In comes my mother – doing her 'yoo hoo' from the front door, carrying her signature wicker basket for her pinny and some shoes she can work in. She's had her hair permed again, which I told her not to, and the moment she steps into my house she sets off an alarm, an alarm which means she's in my space and in my face. I simultaneously detest the intrusion and welcome the help and her company – which is exactly how I felt when I first left home to go to university and she came to visit. Spookily nothing has changed.

Curiously she doesn't notice my purple hair. Was expecting a BIG reaction. She talks to me non-stop – endless friendly harmless questions – how are the girls? Have we sorted out a holiday yet? Did I read about the new vitamins for the change? Would I like her to get me some? Did I remember Aunty Brenda's birthday? I have no right to be niggled by it all (mind you she does keep putting the washing-up liquid away under the sink despite me telling her not to every time she comes round –

which is enough to niggle anyone) – but I get all curt and short
with her, move rooms, leave her in the kitchen, and generally
feel bad about it all. She gets stuck into the ironing, and I snatch
something out of the basket saying it must be ironed inside out,
or I'll do that one it's a bit precious or something really catty and
ungrateful, then when she gets out the apple crumble she's
made for us with her own apples I say I'll put it in the freezer,
which of course is like saying I don't want it at all. I can't help it.
It's like I'm programmed to be niggled by her.

Once in a while I'll tell her some news spontaneously – like
that YOUNGEST has got her Grade 3 piano, or I had some
triumph at work, and she looks proud. As if that was what she
was waiting for, that was the point of it all. All the insolence and
the bad temper she takes from me day in, day out are worth it,
fuels her motherly love until the next time I decide I can let out a
bit of news, or tell her about something on my mind. Until then
she has to put up with all the huffing and puffing and generally
not being appreciated. So this is how motherhood ends up –
with a huffy daughter with her own life and her own family and
little thought or thanks for the years of slog and hard work she
put in for me.

And of course it doesn't take me long to work out that this is
how my own daughters are going to be with me. Already are.
And how I am going to be with them. I already speak her
language. I say something like 'mind how you go', or 'wrap up
warm'. I am her. I even quite like lavender talc. It just happens –
there is nothing you can do about it. Sometimes motherhood
really stinks.

Since my father died she has become more needy, despite the
newfound social life, so now she is not only irritating but
demanding too. Widowhood is one of those things that people
are simply not very sympathetic about. It's statistically so likely,

so predictable, that when it happens the world is sympathetic for about a month, then expects women to get on with it. As she leaves she says, 'By the way your purple hair looks ridiculous.' I feel small. Cut down to size. Like I would have done at 13. Job done.

To Do
Is GOM's life insured?
Be nicer to my mother
Use public library more
Call hairdresser
Flog some things on eBay

February 7th

People at work pretend to like my hair, saying it makes me look cool, or funky; that's what they say, those are the words that are coming out of their mouths, but I can tell they think otherwise. Imagine there are one or two emails with 'get her' or 'you'd think at her age she'd know better' type messages that are a bit of a giggle. They think I look a bit dysfunctional, am wondering whether in fact I am a bit dysfunctional, but if I am, maybe I can blame it on the change and no one will be in the least surprised, hurrah. Stupid all-day meeting at work with a lot of talk about 'synergy' and 'team building' and 'cascading of responsibility'. Something about having to send out a new message. Jocasta used the word 'zeitgeist' and I think even she has no idea what it means.

Found myself in meeting thinking about all the little jobs I have to do at home like sorting out the freezer, buying loo rolls and the mould on the shower tiles that need scrubbing, then got even more bored and daydreamed about getting home and sorting my wardrobe out into colours like in the article in *Prima* magazine I read at the dentist's. It feels like if my sock drawer was sorted, if the airing cupboard was all folded up like a Benetton shop and the glasses were sorted into sizes and nice neat lines, then the rest of my life would fall into place, and I would be entirely happy, calm and sorted. And the busier I get and the more work-type work I am given, the more obsessed with getting home organised military fashion I become. It is a cruel combination and can only lead to dusting at 3am or writing a shopping list on the loo. Both of which I am entirely capable of doing.

The meeting seems to go on for hours and hours and hours. That's because it does go on for hours and hours and hours, with virtually nothing achieved it seems to me; and still the Danish pastries sit in the middle of the table, untouched, since to take one would be to admit to the assembled company that you want a Danish pastry more than you want to say anything in the meeting, which obviously is the case for all of us, but none of us dares be the first. Apparently, according to wonder boss Jocasta, you have to 'harness the energy and deflect it creatively into company core'. Going to be tricky to write that lot down on a flip chart without laughing out loud.

chuckle

mutter

snigger

synergy
zeitgeist
cascading
of
responsibility

TO DO
Form for school trip to France
Put breadmaker in attic
Get damp sorted in spare room

February 8th

ELDEST is learning to drive. GRUMPY OLD MAN and I go to buy cheap-as-chips second-hand car. All I really want to know from the irritating salesman is how many seats does it have? Has it got those nice things that you put your drinks in to stop them spilling on the motorway? Has it got central locking? And how much is it?

You can see they've had nothing to do for hours. The showroom has been empty all morning. You can see they've been looking up in the *Daily Mail* what to watch on telly tonight and reading about hot totty. And so you are a captive audience. And they think a grumpy old couple, nothing better to do, probably only a nearly new sale to organise, or some grouting to do, nothing important, and so they make a meal of it. Take their time, bore you rigid.

'Yes, I see,' I say, hoping he realises that I want him to shut up, but he sees this as a cue to tell me more. On and on and on about it all, and the price and the book price and the road holding and the previous owners and you know it's all lies

TO DO
LIST OF JOBS
FOR GOM

anyway. At least he's not trying to flog you the apricot-coloured one outside on the forecourt. You'd have to be really stupid to drive that one home.

Buying a car still feels like it's the kind of thing your dad should be doing. The car was definitely my father's area. In the old days, when my mother and father were young, the male and female roles were extremely well defined: washing and ironing was my mother's job, along with cooking and cleaning, whereas putting up shelves, paying the bills, and driving and keeping a nice car was my father's. You could argue that the delineation was unfair, but it was clear-cut. Now in our house what seems to have happened is that I've gone out to work full time, but I've retained responsibility for all the things my mother was in charge of as well. OK my husband knows how to cook, and is entirely amenable to putting the wash on . . . but he has to be reminded And the old traditional male areas such as filling up the car and washing it, now that we drive too, have come into the female area of responsibility on top of everything else. Which accounts for why I am in a big filthy mood so much. That's my excuse.

It strikes me that the division of domestic work and responsibility is a source of great irritation and tension in our house. Maybe I could approach this like I am constantly telling people to at work. Like it's a management problem. Make it like a job description, so that people in the family can be clear about where their responsibilities start and end, and so there can be more clarity about who does what and when. I start to make a mental list of some of the things around the house that drive me mad, and some rules that if followed by all family members would alleviate my grump. It'll give you an idea of some of the stuff I carry around in my head, and it might explain why I am sometimes – OK often – in a bad mood.

RULES OF THE HOUSE

When coming into the house please check feet for mud and DO NOT wipe mud in great chunks all over the front doormat.

Please DO NOT put rubbish next to the kitchen bin; either it's IN the bin or it's OUT of the bin.

Put out printed card that says IMMERSION HEATER ON when you switch it on, you will remember to switch it off later.

Please empty the kitchen bin every morning

When eating ice-cream put back in the freezer (with top on).

When leaving living room please take mugs and glasses and plates with you – preferably to the kitchen.

Please put away clean washing placed on your beds not let them get creased up again on the floor.

Please rinse plates before putting in dishwasher as it's the third time I have had to get the plumber in to sort it.

Please leave my pile of change alone and do not nick it for parking or dinner money.

Please put DVDs and CDs back in their covers

Please after use make your own bed.

Put your shoes away not in the middle of the room.

Please put sign saying IMMERSION HEATER back in airing cupboard when you have switched it off again for the next person to use.

THANK YOU

Starting this list (it is only the tip of the iceberg incidentally) has made me realise how much domestic mess and muddle I carry around in my head (and how obsessed I am with the immersion heater). No wonder I am in a bad mood.

GRUMPY OLD MAN manages not to carry any of this around in his head at all. He doesn't have to nag the girls about any of the above, because it simply doesn't matter to him. If there is a pile of rubbish by the kitchen bin he doesn't care, doesn't even notice it, which means he wafts through life and the house oblivious, and seems constantly in a good mood. **Maddening.**

To Do
Be more chilled about housework
Buy new black doormat
Loo wipes
Find electrician to put in automatic
          immersion switcher-on thing

February 9th

Went into town and spotted v. expensive moisturiser cream I read about. It's supposed to be totally and utterly effective on the wrinkle front. Helped myself to a great dollop of the tester in perfume department and smeared it under my eyes, scary woman there in an instant asking if I am interested in buying some. Well, I might be. How much is it? £200 a pot. She had to repeat it. Apparently it has some special ingredient in it which is unique to skin care, uniquely effective at zapping wrinkles, and when she told me what it was I couldn't stop laughing, because the special ingredient is what a table full of marketing gurus would obviously put in a tub that they wanted to flog people like you and me for £200 a pop. The special ingredient is – wait for it – caviar!

To Do
Buy stain remover for coffee table in lounge
Loo wipes
Brasso
E45 cream

February 10th

The snowdrops are coming up. Like magic. Next year when the snowdrops do their magical appearance ELDEST will be gone to university. I sob on the way to work and wonder where her childhood went and what life will be like when her washing isn't in the basket, the house isn't covered in her cereal bowl trail, her bed is permanently made and we look forward so to her Sunday evening phone calls with news and occasional visits – what I need is a hobby to take my mind off it all.

To Do
Book holiday
Self-raising flour
Library
Bin liners
sock drawer sorters

February 11th

The world has gone Valentine's Day mad. There's a *Metro* free paper big spread on what you can buy your partner, and among the chocolates and fru fru nightdresses and knickers is a 'sex toy', as they put it, which looks like a cross between a Henry Moore sculpture and a car jack. Am overcome with embarrassment and curiosity at the same time. There are other people looking at it on their way to work too, I can see because we are all reading the same free paper. I imagine if you did go in for such a thing the worry would be that it had an electrical funny turn and you ended up having to call an ambulance, or your loved ones would find you electrocuted in a very embarrassing position, probably quite literally . . . It wouldn't be worth the risk.

I love being a mother x x

February 12th

Hideous bloke at work with personal hygiene problem lingering in the office telling jokes. He's from post room. I feel quite sorry for him, but really jokes are so not funny. Jokes send me into a panic. I often don't understand them, which is not because I am Miss Innocent or Miss Prissy but more that I just don't find them funny. I get in a panic. When should I laugh? Is this the punch line? Or is that? I have to wait for someone else to start laughing. Oh God! He told one about a one-eyed Eskimo that lasted about 20 minutes. I get all hot and bothered and feel trapped and want to kill him. Everyone else drifted off back to their computers and left me lumbered with him, like he might be my sort. I am going to tell the next person who asks me if I have heard the one about . . . that no, I haven't, and no, actually I don't want to hear it.

A sunny but freezing cold February day, I have started to resent being stuck in the office on sunny days at work, resent not being able to be outdoors, which is God's way of telling me that at my age I should probably be thinking of retiring. No chance until I have saved up for proper pension plan and/or face lift and Botox programme.

To Do
Have sex MORE
Book token for Uncle Joe
Look into my pension

February 14th

Every year is the same. He leaves it until he comes home from work, which means that I am in a potentially cross mood all day, I mean a girl needs flowers on Valentine's Day. And not from the Shell garage. Mind you, you wouldn't want it to go the other way – get a huge bunch of flowers from a really posh florist, or a romantic surprise weekend in Paris – not after 18 years of marriage – could only mean he was having an affair so best be grateful for normality. Even my mother has had a card. Rang me up to tell me, as though I'm her new best friend. Sounded like she'd been at the sherry. Feel ridiculously a bit jealous.

Find Valentine card under my pillow. Hadn't looked this morning. Apologise.

To DO
Book hairdresser
Dental check up for girls
VET- dog wormers
Library opening hours

February 16th

I'm becoming the kind of woman who shops in supermarkets and dumps her unwanted goods anywhere. Boot polish by the cream crackers, hair mousse by the fresh meats, I don't care. They make so much money out of me and everyone else I figure it'll give them all something to do. If there's a queue at the checkouts I ask someone who seems slightly less gormless than the others and looks older than 12 if they could possibly open another lane, which is code for I'll cause a riot if not. And why don't any of them know what anything they sell actually is? Don't pretend you know what sundried tomatoes are when you don't, young man. Don't direct me to the freezer section when I ask for some Halloumi cheese.

To DO
Find out evening class timetable
Go to library sat am

February 17th

Finally go to library and tick it off my 'to do' list with a
flourish and a lot of scribbling out – almost tearing the paper.
Must be five years since I set foot in the place – when we used to
sit on the little chair in the children's section when the girls were
small, when they were still mine, when they still adored me . . .
still liked me even. Like most public libraries ours has an
overwhelming smell of flatulence, mixed with wet coats, and is
full of tramps sheltering from the rain and a lot of people who
look like they just got made redundant and are scanning the jobs
pages on-line to save buying them.

I ask if they have the latest Jamie Oliver, and that I'd heard
that if they didn't they would have to order it for me since I am a
fully paid-up member of community and library to boot.
Unsurprisingly it is not that simple. They have to try all the local
libraries first to see if they have it, and then, if they do, you have
to wait your turn in the queue to see if someone returns it. Plus it
costs 90p to do a search. Libraries are evidently not the sort of
place for an impatient cow like me. I turn my attention to the
videos, something educationally sound for the girls, tease them
away from *America's Top Model* and the annoying Paris Hilton. I
browse along the carousels – I was hoping for all those nice
David Attenborough series, or something on architecture, or
even a really good film like *Love Actually*, I was thinking *The
Office*, *24* series 3, that sort of caper, but what they have is a
miserable selection of things which might tip you over the edge.
Live alone and have an evening in with one of these and you
might just lose the will to live. *T'ai Chi for Arthritis* . . . *Farming
Equipment in Yesteryear* . . . *Painting with Acrylics* . . .
Understanding Falconry – you'd have trouble shifting these at a

car boot sale. Lug them into the Oxfam shop and they'd make you take them back to the car in disgust.

The romance section catches my eye. The books have the kind of binding I recall that my mother and her sister used to take to Bournemouth on holiday, Mills and Boon type stories but obviously not so 'common'. The sort of thing I should be reading too – perhaps – a woman of my age and standing . . . some of them in large print . . . even better. The titles are marvellously atmospheric: *A Bride by Accident*, *In His Tender Care*, *His Virgin Secretary*, *His Very Personal Assistant*. On second thoughts, they sound a bit dodgy. Maybe my mother was reading a bit of soft porn on the quiet.

I borrow five books which all seem like they could lead to some hobbies. A woman of my age should start to have hobbies for when the kids leave home, your husband is too old for any hanky-panky and your sciatica is playing up. Some crochet. Some needlepoint, or some nice gentle yoga exercises for the over forties and some nice easy rambles for a Sunday afternoon. They weigh a ton, but I feel sorted.

Get a parking ticket outside the library. Could have bought three books of my very own for the price . . . including the latest Jamie Oliver. Instead of which I have borrowed five books I sort of half want to read or feel I might find useful. Which is very bad indeed. But worse than that the mess it has made on the windscreen is horrendous. Get home and go inside and get soapy water and green scourer and give it some elbow grease. Only half of it shifted.

TO DO
MAKE A NOTE WHEN BOOKS ARE DUE
    BACK ON KITCHEN CALENDAR
Pay parking fine

February 20th

My periods are going berserk again. One month there's
nothing at all and then the next I am virtually housebound;
sitting on someone's cream sofa would be out of the question. I
go to the doctor and she says I am peri-menopausal. Which
sounds like it's something to do with Perry Como. Then she asks
me to get on the scales. I hate the way she wears her cardigan
draped over her shoulders, makes her look stuck-up and pleased
with herself. She sends off some blood tests to see how near I am
to the change, and shoos me away with a prescription for some
sanitary towels that look like French bolster pillows and are as
large. If I wore some skinny jeans I'd look like a transsexual on
the front bottom bit.

She tells me to do a daily menstrual mood chart and put on
all details of periods for the next four weeks and come back to
see her for the results of the test. Plan to make it juicy reading
for her, pity I can't put in samples.

Spend a jolly half-hour filling in mood and menstrual chart
first of all retrospectively over last 48 hours. Just put block
letters all through both days saying IN A FILTHY FOUL MOOD
FROM MORNING TILL NIGHT AND THEN ALL NIGHT TOO.
Am becoming more of an adolescent than my teenage
daughters.

Obviously I can't do this on all 30 days and anyway it would
make for very boring reading indeed. Might have to make up
some really chirpy days. As in 'had a lovely day today making
quilt and walking in the fresh air'. Yes, right.

February 21st

Making the beds this morning, doing my daily bad-tempered Mary Poppins impression, folding-towels-and-putting-things-away routine that no one else does or cares about, and I find YOUNGEST's diary. Under her bed. It's a Dalmatian one with a lock and key, and it's locked. Which of course instantly makes me want to read it. I prised it open enough to want to see more but not enough to know whether I need to proceed or not. Lots of text words like 'I h8', and 'hitting on someone', which for those of you who don't have teenage daughters means flirting to you and me, and I think I could read the end of 'condoms' because I could see 'oms', and wonder what else it could be – 'pompoms'? 'toms' as in 'tomatoes'? I don't think so. Am I the sort of mother who finds the key and reads her daughter's secret diary? Not sure. Will ponder.

To Do

Have I put date of library books back on calendar?

Ink remover for stain on bedspread

Post catalogue returns

Primrose oil

February 25th

Go to hairdresser's for highlights to cover up stupid childish purple daubings, and while I'm at it get the grey bits covered up again with highlights. Highlights are now crucial rather than simply desirable because of the spreading grey bits. Why it takes so long is beyond me. Faffing on with bits of silver paper, cooking under something that looks like it was in Bleep and Booster, you're there so long shifts come on and go off again. Most of the time you can see they are thinking, 'This woman is in her late forties . . . like it matters what her hair looks like, anyway.' And they will insist on talking to you. All of them, the one that washes your hair, the one that 'takes you through', the colour technician (impressive job title or what?) and the hairdresser herself. Talk to you about the kind of things that you can predict to the letter. Are you going somewhere special tonight? Where are you going on your holidays? Are you all ready for Christmas? I want to shout, 'SHUT UP SHUT UP SHUT UP! I don't want to talk to you, I talk to people all day. I just want to read the paper and anyway to be honest I don't feel like telling you about my holidays; you are eight and a half and look silly with your hair extensions and you've been out the back having a fag when you pretended you were mixing the colour, so shove off.' I take newspapers in, I take work in, sometimes I take my laptop in . . . but still they ask me if I'm going anywhere nice. Not that being rude would

Return library books

Find library books

do you any good, they'd only take revenge and leave your colour on for too long.

Hairdressing salons aren't the female refuge they used to be. Today there's a bloke in an orange Day-Glo jacket who looked like he must be coming into the salon to tell us about a gas leak, but no, he checked in after me and to my astonishment he was at the next station with his own silver foil having highlights. Feel disorientated. Not sure I have ever slept with a man who's had highlights just like mine, not ones to cover up the grey obviously, but some blond highlights, or a tattoo. Better get a move on.

TO DO
Find a library book to check on which date
due back and put note in diary
                                    and at work
Buy posh hair conditioner

Return library
books

February 27th

    Told Jocasta that I was working at
home. Doing my visuals for the presentation next week, but
spent a happy two hours cleaning the Venetian blinds in the
bathroom with new special gadget from Lakeland. Happy happy
happy! Will have to catch up tomorrow.

TO DO
Venetians downstairs too
Buy screw-top bulbs for bathroom
Take back school uniform —
                        Skirt wrong size

March

March 1st

YOUNGEST opens front door wearing shortest skirt to date, more of a belt than a skirt, says she's going 'shopping' . . . which judging by the outfit involves meeting some boys. She's spent the morning soaking in the bath, straightening her hair and yelling at me for – apparently – hiding her favourite top. Which I haven't. But I might hide that skirt, or better still ruin it in the wash, or iron it and singe it 'by mistake', oops silly me. Like my own mother did. Only I would cover my tracks better. My mother denied confiscating my red patent stack-heeled slingbacks in the 1970s, the ones that made me look like Dave Hill in Slade . . . and I believed her, till I found them in the dustbin. And now here I am, one generation on, and I find myself shouting that I will not allow her to go out like that, and when she asks why I say she looks common. Which is just what my mother would have said to me. And when she ignores me and says I am sooooo sad, I resort to telling her she can't because I say so. So much for all the anger management sessions at work.

For some reason at home I am incapable of using any of those skills, because I am resorting to just yelling at the top of my voice to tell her not to. With no visible effect at all, since she goes out in the outfit just the same. Must be more to this than meets the eye.

Find library books

Decide to have another go at getting into her diary once the coast is clear. Get the pliers out and, hey presto, I'm in. Feel ashamed of myself intruding into her private thoughts in a way that I utterly disapprove of but apparently cannot override. In fact there is nothing but harmless girly talk about her friends (and enemies) and some boys she fancies. Shock horror. The 'oms' that I thought was the end of 'condoms' is in fact the end of 'Toms house', 'Toms hair', 'Toms friend', 'Toms part in the play' . . . So yes, there is a boy involved but it all sounds reassuringly harmless. I am more disappointed that she still can't do apostrophes than anything else. Stupid idea of mine to crack it open, and now I have to try to get the lock back on before she notices.

TO DO
Find out about transcendental
            meditation classes
Ring homeopathy place
Talk to school – haven't they done
            apostrophes yet?
And when are they doing contraception?

March 2nd

Jocasta sends us all down to head office in London for big all-day meeting. Audrey and I sit next to one another on the train. Audrey is even older than me. Lovely Audrey from accounts: I look at her and think that frankly she's looking a bit older, a bit ragged round the eyes, she's got the wrong shade of pink lipstick on, and a lot of it, and a jade-coloured top that if I'm honest doesn't do her any favours, but then why would anyone in their right mind buy any clothes in the colour jade? She does that flappy thing and mouths 'hot flush' conspiratorially so the others can't hear, like it's meant for me, which it is, and I feel like moving seats and saying, 'Look, I'm not as old as you, Audrey, I'm still young, still with it' and realise how childish and futile and frankly how inaccurate that would be. Audrey, the very name defines her as middle-aged, as does mine; truth is we are in it together, there is no fighting it, we are the oldies, we are old girls, we need to embrace it and get on with it.

Doesn't stop us having a good old bitch about Jocasta though, especially the ridiculous outfit she has on today for head office. Slitty skirt, heels that are so high she will be in agony, and bare legs which can only lead to heel blisters and some tragic plasters tomorrow. We decide to look out for them. She is holding forth on the train, the others are laughing a little too readily at her jokes, and Robin is going completely over the top fawning away and virtually sitting on her lap. Ghastly display. Sometimes being older means you can rise above such things, pretend you haven't heard or go for a wander and say your back's playing up. Looking forward to seeing Jocasta show off in front of her boss and having to do some sucking up herself.

Find library books

Get there and the meeting is full of people trendier and younger than Jocasta. But Boss's boss is in fact about my age. Felt good. Jocasta struggling when asked by him to kick off brainstorm on noisy ideas for next quarter. Saw her go a bit red and flounder for her notes. Worth the trip alone.

TO DO
Send some suggestions to Jocasta's boss
Heel plasters for YOUNGEST
Buy new lipstick

March 3rd

ELDEST is applying for universities. The prospectuses are arriving daily. She favours Aberdeen. We were allowed to drive her up for Open Day. The place was so far north I thought we'd drive off the end of the country and fall into the sea. Hours and hours and hours of driving even beyond Edinburgh. So this is how much she wants to get away from us.
We get there and it is perishingly cold, with a bitter gale blowing off the sea and a constant drizzle. Despite all this, the place is absolutely charming. That's to say what I was allowed to see of it was, because obviously we were forbidden from getting out of the car unless strictly necessary. As a teenager you suddenly become aware that the one thing that gives away your identity, says more about you than the clothes you wear, the posters you hang in your room or the music you play . . . is your parents.
The whole day whisks me back to my own student days – the little identical windows in hall, with the same curtains, the

study bays in the library, the refectory, the union bar . . .
University was where I decided who I was, decided who I was
going to be in adulthood, and she will do the same, without us,
without me, and that of course is the point. This will be her
home. This will be where I will need to imagine her, laughing,
throwing her first dinner parties, chatting, having coffees with
all those new people she is going to meet from all over the
world, swapping life stories. Soon she will have a life of her own
away from us. Could sob . . . sob that I didn't drop everything
when she was little, when we snuggled up in bed, when we sang
'Wheels on the Bus', when she loved to sit on my lap, when her
little hand held mine and we did fairy kisses and she fell asleep
in my arms and went all floppy in her little lemon-coloured
Babygro, the one with the ducks on that I loved. What was I
thinking of carrying on with my stupid career, missing out on
time I could have had with her then, before it was too late? It
feels hard to be a working mother when your nest is emptying.
But I can't imagine that mothers who stayed at home find it any
easier. The truth is your main purpose in life – your children –
eventually leave home. You knew that at the beginning, but it is
still going to take a lot of getting used to.

To DO
Sort out memorabilia and photo album
        for ELDEST
Look into top-up fees
Save money

Return library
books

March 5th

ELDEST is now learning to drive but taking her out with the L plates is challenging on the nerves. It all seems to be going so well and then we come down a hill and she slightly misjudges how near we are to the kerb, then overcompensates and just misses an oncoming vehicle by a fraction of an inch. She does this just about every time. And she goes so fast. Young people seem to be so overconfident about everything. I spend the whole time telling her to slow down. Something has rewired in my brain – I find everything, absolutely everything terrifying. Even the car wash gives me the heebie-jeebies, last time I stood at the side rather than stay in the car, dashed out at the last minute once I'd got the money in and slammed the door quick as quick and jumped out of the way – which was infinitely more dangerous than sitting inside and risking fatal crushing by brushes. I should retrain as a Health and Safety officer, would be top of the class.

My father taught me to drive and I think about him a lot. It's a year almost to the day that he died; we've done the round of the seasons, the birthday, Christmas, and naturally it still hurts like hell. He loved his car. With his Roy Orbison cassettes, his Elaine Paige tapes, and most important it was a refuge to smoke in. Years and years after he was not allowed to smoke in the house, he smoked in the car. Secretly of course, except the Nissan Micra always smelled of Benson and Hedges and so it was obvious where my father did his smoking. Which probably explained why he was so amenable to running errands for my mother. I loved my father. He blew me kisses – I wish he could still.

TO DO
Call Mother about lighting a candle
at the Abbey
Stick down carpet
— that is sticking up on the landing

March 8th

My trusty Psion Organiser that has all my contacts on has been playing up for a while. Every time I turn it on it tells me refer to back-up batteries, and I changed the batteries twice but it still sends me the silly message. Obviously I am always too busy to take any notice. But this morning I turned it on and it didn't do anything. I mean it didn't give me the tragic little reminder, or anything, just a blank screen.

I run out to get yet more AA batteries and change them, and then I turn it on and there is the familiar grid. Phew. Thank goodness for that. I think, well really what I should do is go and buy a Blackberry or whatever it is that everyone has, or I should go and try to download all the information on to my computer as I tried to do about four times while I still knew where the manual was and vaguely remembered where the connection lead was, but it failed because it sent me a stupid message. That was irritating and incomprehensible in equal measures. Yes I could do that, and then I would never have to worry about losing all my contacts again . . . except this time when I try to open my first contact a new message comes up that says: NO ITEMS IN FOLDER. Not seen that one before. Try a few other names, the diary, the jotter, nothing. *Nyet*. Nothing. No addresses at all.

I drive straight to John Lewis, virtually sobbing, and nice man on Electrical who is the oracle of all technical knowledge turns it over and asks, 'When was the last time you changed the back-up battery?' 'You mean the batteries . . . I keep changing them, they don't make any difference.' 'No, the back-up one – this one, that looks like a ten-pence piece.' And he opens an entirely different compartment. 'Oh never.' 'And you've had it for two years? Well, you've been lucky. Usually it sends you messages saying you have to refer to the back-up battery.' To warn you that this might happen.

Oh God!

I log on to the website at home for help. Of any sort whatsoever. And it is worse than bad, worse than annoying or irritating or the sort of website I have to get teenage daughter to sort out for me. It is a Dead website. Dead because it says, Psion Organisers are no longer manufactured, this helpline is no longer live, there follows a list of frequently asked questions with some answers. In other words it says, 'Tough luck, sonny, you have goofed up and now we are selling much more efficient, and for that read more expensive, PDAs – whatever that means – so wise up and buy one and chuck your Psion in the bin.'

I do what everyone does in this situation and throw myself at the only person I know who understands all this stuff, Paul from IT at work, the man who has many women throwing themselves at him for help (but only in the office). He says he'll have a go, a little flicker of hope opens up in my mind, he presses some of the buttons, uses the pointy thing, then says, 'Have you tried switching it on and off again?' OK, so he doesn't know any more than I do really. 'Have you changed the batteries?' 'Yes.' 'It's dead then.' At least with a Filofax you had the clear tangible bits of paper that you could photocopy, that you could keep in your drawer at home. Now I am sunk. Well and truly stuffed. Never mind all the work contacts – what about the woman who does the bit of ironing for me, the man who does all that cheap reupholstery and the window cleaner? So now I am back to square one. It's all very well inventing all these sophisticated little computer things for you to copy all your life into, but when they die on you, you are stuffed. Why can't someone invent something useful, like one-size tights that fit anyone at all, chocolate that takes your wrinkles away or some calorie-free Kettle chips?

TO DO
Buy chocolate
            (black organic free trade)

March 10th

Library books are due back. I know that because I put more notes to myself all over the house than were strictly necessary or normal. Trouble is I failed to make a note of what I had done with the books themselves, and can only find four out of the five. *Teach Yourself Italian* is missing. I wouldn't mind if I had read it cover to cover and had mastered beginner's Italian – I haven't opened it. Can't even remember seeing it lying anywhere. Ransack study, ransack kitchen and resort to (pointlessly) looking in laundry room, like someone might have taken it in there to put it on to wash. Look again in living room.

The other four books sit on the hall table and scream self-loathing and disappointment, because guess what? I didn't trace my family tree, and I didn't start quilting. Well, that's not true, I did start quilting, I went to the

Return library books

sewing shop (what a haven of tranquillity that is, in my next life I'm going to run a nice sewing shop with a lot of gingham and felt squares – I think I must have been their first customer in three weeks) and bought £40 worth of silks, £10 of needles and £5 worth of patterns with the intention of making a gorgeous family-heirloom-type quilt for ELDEST to take away to university to remind her how much I love her. Except it was all much harder than I had anticipated, and the squares didn't come out quite square and I threw it all in the corner in a fit of temper like a four-year-old. No one had explained that quilting, like most hobbies, requires time and patience – neither of which I have, but which is I suppose the point of them.

I get to the library and there's a spread of books on local history which looks so dull I might usefully think about them when I wake up with racing overactive brain in the night with a hot flush and can't get back off again. She puts the ones I bring back through her electronic beeper thing. Sure enough she knows the *Teach Yourself Italian* one is missing. In the old days I might have got away with it, blagged my way out of it with a lot of stuck-up huffing and puffing, but not any more; everything is computerised. Probably got me on CCTV carrying the blooming thing out a month ago.

The fine is 54p per day. I say I think she's got it wrong. Must be 54p a week. No it's not wrong, it is 54p per day. How else do they deter people from losing books? In a mere 13 days I will probably have clocked up the equivalent of buying it new. And judging by the illustrations it was published in the seventies. So now I have to ransack the whole house.

To Do
Get hobby

Find library books

WINDOW OF
CALM 20 mins

MARCH
7 MONDAY

PEOPLE ON
MOBILES ! aaarghh

In a FILTHY MOOD
ALL DAY

★★ ANOTHER
HOT FLUSH

8

Old girl counting
change out in a
queue getting in
my way COULD HAVE
SHOT her

BLOWN
LIKE A
PRESSURE
COOKER !

JANUARY 11

March 13th

Back to the doctor's for the results of the blood tests. She's got
my bulging notes out and she asks me how I am, which seems a
bit pointless since she's my doctor and if she really wants to
know the answer
I can give her a long list of niggles, concerns and intermittent
problems to keep her occupied all day . . . I get my mood diary
out. She looks at it like it's about to burst into flames.
As if she's reluctant to handle it or touch it at all. I'd gone a bit
over the top here and there with all the capital letters saying IN
A FILTHY MOOD ALL DAY, and WENT INTO TOWN AND OLD
GIRL COUNTING CHANGE OUT IN A QUEUE GOT IN MY WAY
AND COULD HAVE CHEERFULLY SHOT HER IF GUNS WERE
LEGAL. She looks a bit shocked. A bit frightened of me . . . and

gets the results on screen. 'Yes, well, your oestrogen levels are slightly lower than average; I wouldn't say you were in the change yet, but you might be heading towards it.'

'Do you mean to say that this is just the beginning? How long does the change usually take?'

'It depends. Can be anything from two to ten years.'
I think my mouth dropped open.

'I think we'll try you on some low-dosage HRT shall we?'

Why do doctors talk to you like you're a four-year-old? Anyone would think I behave childishly.

Go to the chemist and pitifully feel like saying they are for a friend, not for me, I am still in the land of the living, still ovulating. It's pathetic. I get them home and open them up. They look remarkably like the pill, as far as I can remember that is, in a one-per-day-type package. Exactly like the pill. Decide to leave them in the bathroom for ELDEST to see. I'd have preferred a pregnancy testing kit, really give her a fright, but this will have to do. She will have to reconsider me as a woman, as a woman with womanly needs and a healthy sex drive.

TO DO
Find out about herbal menopause things
Call Maggie to ask her about water
 retention tablets she was raving about

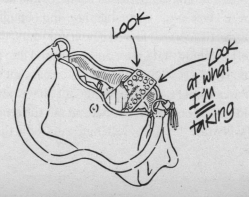

March 18th

Am beginning to wonder whether the HRT is female Viagra by mistake. Sudden rush of female hormones. Feel so horny I can hardly sit down. And the jeans! They mean I am almost permanently on heat. GOM getting a bit tired of it all. Well a bit tired full stop. If only I could show off a few carpet burns, a few love bites, that'd really make the people at work sit up and look. I fancy just about everyone. Builders have stopped noticing me but I've started to notice builders, men in uniform, men on the side of the road in vesty-type things, men with tattoos, men covered in dust from construction work – it's all a bit of a worry. I've started watching *Top Gear*. Got a bit of a crush on Jeremy Clarkson, quite a lot of a crush in fact. More worrying – I have a crush on the other one with the funny long ex-hippy frizzy hair and appalling dress sense. That has to be chemically induced.

To Do
Find new odd-job man

March 20th

Something happened today that I had absolutely no control over. I was at the vegetable shop and I bought a big bag of birdseed. We've had a bird table for years, the people before us left it behind and I have only ever used it to put the peg basket on. GOM occasionally puts a few crusts out on it and jabbers on about seeing a yellowhammer but I have never really seen the point of it before. Got home and put the seed out.
I will draw the line at watching Bill Oddie though.

To Do
Get hobby
Buy bird book
Sweep terrace by bird table

March 21st

Found *Teach Yourself Italian* in the neat pile next to bed by
other books I keep meaning to finish . . . or start. Someone has
either sneaked it on the pile because they had secretly stolen it,
or I forgot to look there and since it is the most obvious place to
keep a book I am planning to read, and don't get round
to, this is a worry. Brain falling apart or
springing holes like a colander.

Find yesterday's
To Do list —
does it have
marjorie's number
on?

March 22nd

Huge hold-up on the motorway on the way to work. Everyone
is so fed up they start to make calls, pick arguments with their
fellow passengers, ring Radio 2 to report the hold-up (so they
must be bored), make lists, send emails, call people they haven't
spoken to for years, or (in my case) start plucking their whiskery
beard in the rear-view mirror. The whole thing takes nearly an

hour. Got to the hold-up to discover it was just road works. I won't be the only one who was disappointed. I mean when you've had the top end of your day capped by one hour you want to see some paramedics at least. Better still some helicopters and air-sea rescue. At least that would have made it sort of worthwhile. Shameful thoughts. No wonder I never win the Lottery, or the Premium Bonds, or even the raffle at school or even anything nicer than the bath salts at a tombola. I simply don't deserve to.

TO DO
call charity shop again to change
    YOUNGEST arrangements for Saturday
Help for DOE bronze award
Put out clothes for charity shop

March 23rd

Jocasta wants me to do a presentation at monthly away day. Called 'Managing Chaos'. Good job we're not talking about real life since my life is – well – chaotic. Says she's calling me on Sunday night with her thoughts about the ground it should cover. Great. Will have to be ready with notes and silly pretentious-sounding ideas for Sunday night. Might put some smart Mozart on in the background, impress her, make my life sound calm and zen and very very sophisticated.

Find BEST OF MOZART CD

March 26th

My presentation looms. Most preoccupied with what I will wear and if I can manage to shift some weight in time. Might have to buy one of those all-in-one corsets. Double chin very very big problem, will have to push my chin up as in very very haughty stuck-up woman with shouty voice.
Might frighten people.

TO DO
Find tax paperwork
Call tax office
Buy sugar substitute stuff

March 27th

The away day looms. Go to Marks to investigate all-in-one corsets and pull-me-ins, and there they are – the beauties – racks and racks of them (so they must be pretty popular which is a comfort), but obviously they're tucked away at the back, far away from the little gorgeous pink-and-lime-green-fru-fru things, far far away from the eyes of men who might stray there by accident. Which suits me fine, I mean you wouldn't frankly want to meet anyone much you know in this neck of the woods. The bra sizes are all up in the telephone numbers . . . DD, FF, GG even . . . and all marvellously scientific – a hundred different functions and designs, pull you in, push you out, push you up, push you all about. All in white, black or a really horrid flesh colour that reminds me of the torso on the side of the pool that they use for lifeguard training. I take one corset to try at home.

Get it home and the trouble begins. They don't tell you whether to step into it and pull it up, or put it over your head and pull the whole thing down over your body, and for once some instructions would be useful. That's spiteful of them. So I go for over the head. The fabric doesn't give, which I suppose is the point . . . so I have trouble getting it over my boobs and get stuck halfway over and what I really need is help. Someone to come in and yank the bottom down over the remaining half of my bust and pull it towards the floor. But a) finding someone willing to get involved in such a scary scene would be problematic, and b) actually venturing out of a locked room in this state would be mad to dangerous. So I yank some more, yank more and more, jumping up and down; the effort of each

yank and the whole thing gets me into a top-of-the-range mither. Phone goes a couple of times and I have to leave it, am utterly indisposed, give myself hot flush, and eventually get it over the boobs and down and then attempt to do it up under the crutch which I assume is the way it stays on.

By definition, this thing is going to have to be tight to do its job, in other words to pull the whole flabby mess of my body in and hold it down and under control. But instead of being made of stainless steel or instead of being the sewing equivalent of flying buttresses, there are three silly little press-studs designed to be done up under the crotch to keep it in place. It's also incredibly difficult to see what you're doing, because it's a sort of up and under manoeuvre, so I have to put my reading glasses on . . . but then when you've got a bit of a midriff you can't really get round to the undercarriage bit as well as you used to be able to do, get one half in place, in a bending your knees sort of semi-pornographic pose and you can't get all three of the press-studs done up, have to make do with two. But of course every time you go to the loo this is going to happen. I could be in the loo for half an hour every time, easy.

Of course it does pull me in quite satisfyingly. In an all-over sort of way, not in a push-all-the-blubby-bits-to-another-area way – but it makes me walk in a slightly different way, like someone just told me some bad financial news or I'd done my back in, or I'd sat down on something that looked like a bit of spit on a chair.

To Do
Call ELDEST's history teacher
EHIC card for history trip? By when?
Safety pins
Panty liners
Silver foil
Kitchen roll

MOTHER'S DAY

It's the last one when both girls are living at home. Next year when ELDEST has gone to university, I will be a semi-unemployed mother, a mother who has been offered what feels like early retirement without actually wanting to retire at all, ever, from the role of motherhood. I remember her smell as a baby, the little vest I took with me on a business trip because it smelled of her; I used it to get myself off to sleep.

Mothers Rule OK

Both girls have worked together to bring me up a boiled egg and some toast, with a flower and a card. We've moved on from home-made tissue holders made from egg boxes, and jewellery cases made from old toilet-roll holders, lamentably. But they give me two lovely cards . . . yet more things to go in my memory box. To be a mother of daughters is ecstatically wonderful, and excruciatingly hard. It doesn't seem fair that I'm the one that made most of the sacrifices (see stretch marks, flabby tummy and the misery that is being a working mother) and it's Dad that is the apple of their eyes. With me it's more complicated, I sort of know them too deeply. With mothers and daughters it's all about patterns, you work yourself ragged running a house, and she turns into hang-it-all-out, chill-out organic housewife and mother with a house full of clutter and plenty of quality time with the kids. Then her daughters will probably do the entire opposite. One thing we're all stuck with is the kind of bond between mother and child that saw women whose children were taken away in the concentration camps actually die of broken hearts.

Mother-in-law calls to thank GRUMPY OLD MAN for the lovely flowers. What a beautiful arrangement he'd organised this year. Didn't like to tell her that it was me not adoring son that had organised it. Felt a teeny bit sorry for her . . .

I get ready for bed with a heavy heart. Notice the pile of earrings on my dressing table where I have lost one of a pair . . . Interestingly, you never lose the ones you don't like much, only the ones you cherish.

To DO
Search back of sofa for earring
Take catalogue stuff back to post office
Horlicks
Organise Easter lunch
Non-stick pan
Call Mother to apologise
          for not seeing her

March 28th

    YOUNGEST calls me at work to ask me where I put her cookery basket, she needs it now. It couldn't just be that she lost it, or can't find it, it is me who has put it somewhere, apparently. Everything is my fault it seems.

To DO
Self-raising flour
Baking powder
Vermicelli
Find cake tin

March 29th

    Monthly away day at work. The agenda is the usual large chunk of your life that you are not going to get back, with nothing achieved or learned:

    You know that you are going to stare at the word 'close' all day, long for it, look out of the window and long to be able to run outside and get the wind in your hair or just some fresh air, because the blue sky thinking and open forums and thinking outside the box will just do your head in because the truth is that you just think it's a total waste of money. It's like all the meetings at work all the time, but one long all-day meeting without a break, without even a chance to nip out and do an errand, and the worst thing is that your real work just mounts up all day as a result. Nothing gets ticked off the list; worse, things get added to it all day. Except curiously the things that get

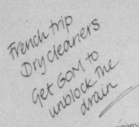

French trip
Dry cleaners
Get GOM to
unblock the
drain

Away Day Agenda

Coffee

09.00–10.30	presentation by Head of Synergy on the future of the company
10.30–11.30	coffee and seminars on blue sky thinking
11.30–12.00	thinking outside the box
12.00–12.30	my presentation on 'Managing Chaos'
12.30–13.00	lunch
13.00–15.00	presentation by Sales on targets
15.00–16.00	open forum
16.00–18.00	seminars on 'seeing problems as opportunities'
18.30	close

I ♥ Steve Martin

I hate meetings

I hate AWAY DAYS!!

aaaughh

added to it are kind of vague like my ten best ideas to Joe in London by next month, or send monthly updates to whole department. The kind of things that you know won't go anywhere, won't amount to anything much.

My presentation gets shunted to after lunch. So that means I have the whole morning to be distracted by the anxiety of it. Despite the fact that I regularly stand up in front of deputations at other companies, because that is my job, standing up in front of my colleagues and boss is infinitely more nerve-racking. I get the silly upset stomach, have it all written out on tragic index cards and underlined bits, go to the loo and say it aloud and it sounds silly like I'm a kid and this is the sort of thing grown-ups do, not me.

I start my presentation and everyone is desperately fighting yawns, there are still two forums to do before the magical much wanted 'close'. What I have to say about managing chaos could be written on a side of A4, OK a post-it note, OK a small post-it note (maybe not one of the little teeny ones you use to mark the page you're on), but much to everyone's surprise I say so. 'I don't use the Powerpoint thing because we've been on that all morning and really who wants to see a visual of a pie chart or a percentage comparison when you can say it in words and have just the same effect. And, guess what, we can all read, so what's the point of showing us a slide with a lot of writing on that you then read out?'

That's one good thing about getting older, you can start to say what you really think, you can put your head above the parapet, you don't care so much what people think of you so you tell it like it is. Managing chaos is all very well, but chaos takes you by surprise; by definition, if you were expecting it then it wouldn't be chaos. So there's not a fat lot you can do to prepare for it, really, other than keep your head and try not to overreact.

I more or less say that. Take about five minutes to say it and everyone looks relieved, actually rather impressed. Fortunately no one was aware that the press-studs holding my undercarriage together pinged open when I picked my pen up from the floor at the beginning and the-all-in-one has been riding up ever since. Ended up partially above the waistband on my skirt, ruched and ruffled up like a horrid Austrian blind for all to see. Good job I wasn't wearing the kind of beach wear my younger colleagues at work do.

To Do
Ring accountant about tax return form
Find tax papers
Call bank
Call building society
Hand in all in one corset thing and find
       receipt and packing and take
                    back to M&S

March 30th

The tax year is coming to an end so the dreaded accountant has to be seen. As usual I fail to do the wretched thing on-line myself and end up paying him to do it for me. His office is old-fashioned, like a time warp out of the 1960s, a lot of shelves with A4 ring files on, some dusty grey filing cabinets and electric fires on the walls. Not exactly state of the art . . . The sort of office where everyone has their own mug, a biscuit kitty, probably a mug tree in the kitchen wouldn't wonder . . . My

accountant has, I imagine, been there for a very long time. We
sit down in his office and he has all the figures in front of him,
and a list of queries a mile long, and starts boring me rigid
talking about PEPs and ISAs and SIPPs and does a lot of
underlinings on a pad and circling things – something about
calendar years and tax years and fiscal risk. I can honestly say
that it's like being in double maths on a Friday afternoon.

Something scary happens. I find myself fancying him. Which
is ridiculous. If you saw my accountant you'd see what I mean:
lovely man, but he has a Disney tie on, fly-away grey hair and is
so near retirement age he's probably allowed to take every
Friday off. The silly fancying thought is just a way of me not
listening to all the tedious things he is trying to tell me, but it
doesn't go away. I start to fantasise about what would happen if
I just leaned over the table and snogged him. Which is a
preposterous notion on many levels, not least of which I have
never even when I was in my twenties and at my most attractive
done anything as daring and as outrageous as snog someone
without having a pretty clear idea that the snog would be
welcome, but the thought doesn't go away. I start to think about
using him as my sex slave. He'd be grateful, let's be honest.

Grateful to the point of astonished, would probably do some really daft things, not go in to work for days on end, hang around me, stalk me. I'd just have to say I like Chanel No.19 and he'd send me a bottle every day, say I shop at Poundstretcher and he'd lurk around there all day on the off chance of catching a glimpse of me. He'd get himself kitted out with contact lenses, and his wife and grown-up children would be baffled but wouldn't guess the reason. He'd go to the doctor and get some Viagra, hide it in the car and be keen to give me full-on sex all night every night. Think I am going bonkers, pull myself together and start trying to listen again.

He gives me a great big telling off about keeping my records in order, the sort of telling-off he gives me every March when his poor staff have had to correct my appalling attempts at filling in the tax return. I go away and start afresh with some labelled shoe boxes, one to put my petrol receipts in, which will last until the next busy period at work. I leave and he is thankfully oblivious to the crush I have developed on him. Maybe we'll elope together, except he'd talk about hedge funds and then I'd get bored and wish I'd stayed with my nice husband.

Am going to have to ask bitch doctor about these HRT pills. What is becoming of me?

To Do
Take GOM out on Saturday night
Corn zappy thing

March 31st

Decide to have a really good clear-out. The sun is shining and it lifts my spirits. The daffodils are out and I tackle the spare room, the shed and the garage, decide to chuck out loads of things that are cluttering up my life, things I haven't used in years. Astonishing how much rubbish you collect that you simply don't need any more. Five bags for the charity shop and a car full – and how! – to go to the tip. I load the car up with bin bags, take two seats out of the back and really have a good clear-out, bag up some garden rubbish too. I spend the whole day on it, really wear myself out. Load it all up and drive to the tip. Feeling purged, feeling as if I'm really achieving something like ticking off everything on five 'to do' lists all at once, a whole week's worth in one day, which means I'm in front, I'm 'straight', got the lists licked, get to the tip and it looks surprisingly quiet.

Barrier down. Closes at 3.30 on a Sunday. Bastards. Now I have to drive back with a car full of crap which I notice is smelling of creosote and mouldy damp carpet that has been sitting by the dustbin for a couple of years minimum, and what's really depressing is that I have to unload it because need the car for school tomorrow. That's not fair. That's negative 'to do' lists with knobs on. That's really really depressing. Get home. Eat chocolate biscuits.

TO DO
Collect all documents relating to income tax form for early fill in NEXT year
Buy more chocolate biscuits
Air freshner for car
Buy more bin bags

April

April 2nd

Am spending far too much time at the mirror. I complain that the girls do this, but I'm starting to be as bad. It strikes me that being middle-aged, going through the midlife crisis so-called, is a bit like being an adolescent – you don't fit in anywhere. Or maybe it's part of the regression towards old age, back to dribbling and a bib and a beaker for your tea in the morning. Thinking about it – numerically this means that I must have regressed further back than adolescence – it's more like being back to the terrible toddler years. I reckon my real regressed type age is about three now and in fact this makes a lot of sense. It would explain all my temper tantrums and rapid mood swings. I'm having trouble with some everyday words, find it hard to remember them, or get them mixed up, calling the cheese grater the chopping board, or the lawnmower the wheelbarrow, I struggle to think of a particular word like 'haphazard' and have to paraphrase it when I can't find it . . . So, in fact, now the flash cards I stuck on everyday things when the girls were toddlers would be an idea for me – one that says 'table' on the kitchen table, 'bed' on the bed and 'window' on the window-pane. It might get out of hand though, I would come to rely on the flash cards, put them on everything like 'my house', 'my car', 'my bunions'. See how it is all sounding like nursery school?

This return to being a toddler also explains my attention-seeking behaviour, like putting purple streaks in my hair, wearing silly bright green coats and my Dr Who multicoloured scarf, big hats and dangly earrings, which are all 'hey look at me, I'm still fun-type statements. Toddlers also need a rest after lunch, which I now do but am not able to take one, making me overtired, fractious and difficult. I don't sleep through the night any more – except, unlike with real toddlers, there is no one to scream at who will get up, give me a cuddle, sing me a song and lull me back to sleep. Maybe all this grump and strop and letting loose on shop assistants who do not serve me within two seconds is one big toddler tantrum. My whole life is one big toddler tantrum. And I could use an afternoon nap in the crèche at work myself, I could use a training beaker for my wine of an evening, I could loll on the sofa watching the telly and it wouldn't drip down my front. Also one of those nice rubber spill-proof dishes for my mashed-up food would mean I could eat in bed, which is where I would really like to spend most of my day. It's all slotting into place . . . except toddlers don't have chin stubble or have to sort the washing into piles.

GET HOBBY

TO DO
Panty liners
call vets
Wine stain removers for white blouse
Take curtains down to wash
Change beds

April 3rd

Standing by coffee station at work and felt completely odd. Like someone had just plugged me into the mains, or a fireball of napalm had rolled down the corridor and was about to engulf me. 'Don't you all feel a bit hot?' I said, but instead of rushing for the fire extinguisher or running away from said napalm fire ball, they all looked a bit sheepish and started to check their emails again. Like they don't do that every ten seconds all day and every day as it is! They had to pretend I hadn't said it because – gosh it was so obvious to them and so not obvious to me – this was my first proper out-in-the-open, in-public hot flush, but unlike any other sexual rite of passage like your first period or your first boyfriend, things to blag to your mates about, to rush about texting your friends, this was the sort of sexual marker best left unmarked, unmentioned and unrecognised. Ignoring a hot flush, though, when you're having one, is not that easy. I mean you can't exactly plunge yourself into a bucket of cold water, which would seem to be the only instant cure, or strip to the waist . . . that might be taking attention-seeking too far. Put hot flush on the mood chart for the

doctor, along with ONE BIG LONG PERIOD scrawled across the week, in case she doesn't pick that up. I'm having one big long dose of pre-menstrual tension from one end of the month to the other. Which is another way of saying one minute I am in a reasonably rational mood and the next I am a seething mass, hysterical bitch making a fuss, or pulling a face or being sarcastic to people doing their job or going about their business. Like the stupid moan I had to the supermarket manager saying, 'Don't you think it would be nice to employ some people in this supermarket that know what some of your products actually are?' The sort of woman who points sarcastically at the notice at the end of the carriage in the train which has a mobile phone on and a sign saying, *Please use with consideration for your fellow passengers*. The one that apparently no one else has read. Because everyone is making stupid calls to people about the dreariest of subjects. How come everyone else seems to have so much more time to kill than I do? On and on and on they drone about what they're wearing on Saturday and what they've been doing all day. The kind of conversations that always end with 'Love you . . . love you'. I just can't let anything lie, anything go, any more, and of course because nothing much embarrasses me any more, there's no stopping me making a fuss.

TO DO
Top up ELDEST's mobile phone card
Find out about relaxation classes
                    at high school

April 6th

Counted five people using their mobiles on way in to work, two of them lorry drivers; tried to take down their numbers but was difficult while driving.

April 7th

Just as ELDEST is about to leave home, GRUMPY OLD MAN is talking about taking early retirement, which is all very well but the net result will be that yours truly might end up being main breadwinner, shit and help, and GOM will be around the house a lot more. Don't know which worries me more. The truth is that, while he is away 8am–7pm five days a week, he is forgiven (a little bit anyway) for not putting the new loo roll on the holder, only taking the laundry basket down when asked and generally making a dog's dinner of anything I asked him to do around the house. But with him at home – then what? I bet I will come home after winning bread to find laundry still in wash basket, no food made, the dishwasher full of clean dishes still, and he'll be sorting out the family holiday album from 1988. None of the little jobs (as my mother would have put it) that I left out on a

TO DO —
Put notebook
in car with pen

list by the kitchen phone will have been done, and he'll be having a nice time. I sense that he will find the newfound freedom exhilarating whereas, during the dollops of time I had at home to look after babies, I was either going to mums and toddlers and listening to other mothers drone on about pram designs or the nearly new sale in order to get my children friends, or I was mopping up sick, or watching *Rosie and Jim* videos while nursing them through chickenpox. He'll probably be on Sky Sports all afternoon.

HOT FLUSHES

He's started to self-delude. As in thinks he is young and hip again. Started playing Coldplay and James Blunt and showing off to the girls about the latest Bono. They look absurdly impressed and maddeningly start to take him a little bit seriously. Any fool can see that the man is a fraud. Underneath he is one of Alan Freeman's pop pickers. Sometimes little things drop out of his mouth that he can't control, like ELDEST talks about Eminem and he thinks it's a chocolate, which is a reality check . . . brings him back to his real age . . . I caught him talking to them about the hit parade yesterday. Back of the net.

To DO
Look into pension plan
Book holiday
MOT due
Receipt for toaster
Buy Coldplay CD

April 9th

GOM has persuaded me to buy a Blackberry. Which until recently I thought was something you picked in September and then made crumbles with, but apparently it's the thing to have gadget wise – and will impress colleagues at work. You can access your emails anywhere, and put all your addresses and important dates in bla bla bla . . . I am so completely hopeless about technological things I regularly point the mobile at the telly, but OLD MAN insists it is easy to operate. Might be for him. Will ponder.

Bird table getting interesting . . . lots of blue-coloured birds and a big black bully on it today. And something dappled that I suppose must be a thrush. Find myself wanting to know the names of them. Suggest I put a shorthand pad by phone so we can all note down the ones we see, and get a Ladybird bird book from Smith's. If teenage girls could tut, their look to me would have been a tut, a trainee tut, like 'Crikey hasn't this woman got anything better to do?'

HOT FLUSH

To DO
Bird book
Join RSPB
Ask IT man at work whether mobile
   will be compatible with my computer

April 10th

Took train to London. Everyone has gone Sudoku mad. I swear two-thirds of the people on the train were doing it. I have trouble with the word Sudoku, the first time I saw it written down I read it as Soduko and now I constantly call it Soduko – can't rewire my brain back to the right one. It's yet another example of me turning into my mother, she had trouble with Richard Branson whom she always calls Richard Branston, and however many times I have corrected her it fails to work. It's like the phrase 'no brainer' which still implies to me that someone is stupid rather than that you don't have to think about something, it's so obvious – I just don't get it.

I am on the 09.38 and pathetically I eat my sandwich immediately the train gets moving. I mean I've had my breakfast – the sandwich is my lunch – but I simply can't be on the move without eating. When I was a kid I was the sort of girl who ate her

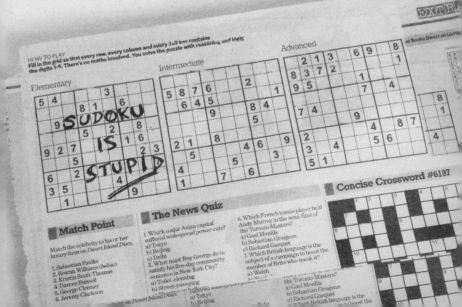

sandwich before the coach had left the coach park for the school trip, which meant I then had only the apple when I was really hungry at lunchtime proper. I suppose greedy would be another way of putting it.

I go to the loo next to the buffet – the one with a funny round door. I think it's the disabled loo because you could get a herd of elephants in it, as opposed to the usual ones which are so small you have to reverse into them and if you have a bag you get it stuck on the handle . . . This one has the strange door which moves very slowly indeed. And it has a ridiculously complicated locking system. You get in and you have to press the button that says 'Close' first then the 'Lock' button inside, and it closes very very slowly while you pretend to do something other than get ready to pull your pants down, and then it lights up a new button saying 'Locked' . . . So I'm on the loo, midstream as it were, and someone obviously touches the 'Open' button from the outside wanting to get in. Despite the fact that I think I have locked it, and the light says 'Locked', the door opens very very slowly indeed, revealing me on the loo. I attempt to stop it opening, but stupid thing is programmed to complete the action very very slowly irrespective of what button you push. So there I sit, slowly revealed on the loo doing a number one. I think the bloke waiting might at least have moved on to another carriage, but when I finally get out he is still standing there. I might know not to trust something as complicated as that sort of fancy closing door. What was wrong with a bolt?

Or a normal door you can slam shut with your foot? See, now I've been on a rant. Breathe . . . It's not good for me. I need a megaphone.

Buy herbal calm remedy

April 15th

The entire world has gone eBay mad. Three people at work today had to break off conversations or meetings to go and put a bid in, or see if they'd bagged something on eBay. It's not like they're buying and selling antiques or Picassos, they're buying and selling old ice skates, or a single mattress or a duvet cover. Have these people got more time on their hands than is properly decent?

April 16th

Decide to have a go at eBay and sell running machine that has been sitting in spare room for four years. Suddenly I can see the point of it. It's basically the same as taking things back to M & S but this way you can take things back when you have used them for a while, or try to get money for all the rubbish in your spare room or cupboard that is annoying you or you have gone off. Stuff that is not nice enough to go into your recycling-presents box. It explains exactly why the whole world has gone eBay mad. Copy down model number and take it in to work; will join the rest of them and pretend I am checking work-type emails but am really buying and selling crap on eBay. The website is easy enough to find – and I key in selling running machines. The number of entries is so large it is in the millions, and get on the list and you soon see that – surprise surprise – the entire world is trying to sell its running machine. When I say the entire world I mean exactly that, because at least the first 20 of the entries of people selling running machines are in Minnesota or Florida or downtown Washington, so the first task is to find running machines in this country to compare price with, and then to sort them down and find one with the same model number as yours. By 11am I had found one similar model and decided how much to sell it for, and had got myself on to the selling part of the website.

Work-work was building up all the time, but undeterred, I put my ad on, and then wonder 'well, this is all very well but what happens if this person from Devon wants to buy it, how do we get it to Devon, and who pays for that, and how do they manage to pay me for it without seeing it first?' Can't help thinking that putting an ad in the local paper is infinitely easier. But on I go. Now for the really time-consuming stuff, filling in your postcode and your birthday and you have to make up another stupid password and user name and code name and it all takes you till lunchtime. Then you have to decide when your bidding starts and ends and put it in 24-hour clock mode so that the whole world (literally) has the chance to bid for your wretched running machine. Have to log off because Jocasta on prowl, and when I get back I have forgotten the new user name and have to start all over again. Virtually whole day spent on it.

To Do
Look out running machine guarantee
                        or receipt
Find other things to flog on eBay

April 17th

No takers for the running machine. Nothing achieved at all. How much time do these people have to waste that do eBay all the time?

April 18th

The nanny state has gone bonkers. Notice in Holland and Barrett they are doing a promotion on brazil nuts, and have a bowl of them for people to help themselves to by the till. Which is lovely. But next to the bowl is a big sign saying 'this product contains nuts'. Never! What next, signs on the roads saying 'contains cars', signs on hospitals saying 'contains illness'? No, we should have some more useful ones like on a Saturday girl, 'contains stupidity', or on a pair of grannie knickers, 'contains no sex appeal'. But the best one yet is one at Bristol airport. You get off the plane, go into the terminal and as you walk in you trigger an automatic voice warning and a hazard triangle with a flashing yellow light, saying 'caution stairs, caution stairs, caution stairs'. Well OK, if the plane had just landed from another planet and aliens whose stairs might frankly be very different were disembarking maybe, but we've all just flown in from Newcastle and as far as I can see a
flight of stairs is a flight of stairs.
The world has gone doolally.

To DO
Put ad in local
paper for
running machine

To Do
Get hobby
Organise girly pamper day with ELDEST
Take Mother to specialist

April 20th

Pottered about for an hour before breakfast which is my daily routine now, so much so that I am wearing slippers and dressing gowns out. And my choice of slippers has become critical: I like  them not too sloppy, yet not too stiff, they need to be functional so that I can take the rubbish out, put a wash on the line and bring some coal indoors in them. Slippers are the new Jimmy Choo as far as I'm concerned. I say that as if I ever had a pair of Jimmy Choos, which obviously I have not. But it sounded good.

Fancy new mobile arrives special delivery. With a manual the size of a novel. But can't find anything that tells you how to answer it. Spend day unable to take any calls, have to email everyone at work to say I have just got fancy new mobile and am not able to answer calls or pick up messages. Sniggers all round.

TO DO
Ask ELDEST to read mobile
                    manual for me

April 24th

Spent whole day at home trying to work the new mobile, on helpline and on website scrolling through the *Getting started* section, and the *Frequently asked questions*, which curiously don't include easily the most frequently asked which must be: 'Why was I so stupid as to buy one of these things in the first place?' The keypad is so small it's the size of a post-it note, and from this I am supposed to be able to text and, call me old-fashioned, make and receive phone calls . . . None of which I have yet mastered. I can't even turn the thing on without putting my reading glasses on, which is not good for my image. Might need to move up a gear, go into bifocals, or resort to one of those silly chains with them on round my neck.

Call computer bloke down the road
Get hobby

April 25th

Get annoyed on phone to fancy mobile HQ, and say I want my money back. Have to parcel it all up, take to the post office and queue, and then pay £10 to send it back registered special delivery. Feel like having toddler tantrum in post office.

BUY FILOFAX

April 26th

Find myself out in town after ten, which is unusual, on a Friday night and am truly appalled. The kind of things that people get up to in full view of everyone on the street after dark are beyond shocking. Standards have quite simply plummeted. And young women seem to be the worst offenders. When our mothers had a night out with the girls, it involved a giggle at a Tupperware party, or a glass of sherry with the Avon lady; now when young women drink with other young women anything goes. The ruder, the drunker, the more debauched the better. And it's not – dare we say it – exactly ladylike.

Women out on the town drunk as skunks is bad enough, but what's with the hen night thing? What happened to girls waiting to be asked? Fluttering their eyelashes? Women at hen nights hunt in packs. For men presumably. They hire horrid stretch limos, lean out of the window, or as I saw the other night, all dressed presumably in their various bridesmaids' dresses, satin

numbers with a lot of bust darts in hideous shades of apricot, burgundy or lemon. Only they're all a bit tight now because they were bridesmaids five years

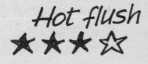

Hot flush
★ ★ ★ ☆

ago, and they get drunk, and their tiaras tip over at an angle and they have to hoik their bridesmaids' dresses up to avoid the slops of beer. Yuk, they make a scary sight . . . presumably to men as well as to everyone else who sees them.

To DO
Find out where ELDEST was last night
New mop head

April 27th

My mother has invited me to her creative writing class end of term do. At her house. She introduces me proudly to everyone and insists I sit next to the guest speaker, a poet from Yorkshire. The first batch of neatly ironed corduroy arrives in very good spirits – early of course. Once you're into your sixties you're early to everything. The women have dressed up their jackets with brooches. There's a lot of beige, some pleated skirts, and they're all wearing comfortable shoes. I pretend I am really too busy to be here at all, but am offering my mother moral support. I fiddle about with the mobile and pretend to check messages etc. – it doesn't pay to make yourself too available for the over sixties. They all seem to be having such a fantastically good time. Joan puts up the cheese and biscuits for the break and nearly wets herself with some in-joke with Dennis, who is dishing out the wine. Giggling, larking about. My mother looks flushed. If you didn't know their age you wouldn't be surprised to see them handing round a joint, and snogging one another. Perhaps they'll wait till my back is turned.

My mother's turn comes round to read aloud one of her creative writing pieces. My heart sinks in anticipation of an embarrassing dollop of her. She stands up. Please no, it's going to be awful. They applaud her supportively. She must be popular.

'My poem is about ageing,' she says. 'Growing old disgracefully.' Her stature surprises me, it's as if I am looking at her for the first time. Her hair looks better cut than usual, her trousers (slacks as she would call them) are nicely cut with a comparatively trendy top covering the bulgy bits. She starts to read this wonderful poem about enjoying being older. And how liberating it is not to have to worry about your waistline, about what people think of you, about your sex life (sex – I don't think I ever heard her use that word before – I think I might have a funny turn). Then she goes on to talk about the mask of old age – that you are still the same young woman or child inside but the world now looks at you with a mixture of pity and indifference. It strikes me that what I'm experiencing in my own midlife crisis is what she has been through and come out of the other end; she has emerged with integrity, grace and a devil-may-care attitude. The group are having a good time. They don't have to worry about spreadsheets, management speak, their careers, their image or what people think of them. They just don't really give a damn. If they want six gin and tonics and some clotted cream, then that's what they'll have. Given up worrying about cholesterol or getting a hangover at their age, sod it. Live for today. Let's go and sit in the garden and potter about in the park . . . Let's not bother to clean the kitchen floor any more. Life is running out and I can't be arsed any more. Let's start collecting margarine pots and plastic bags. Old age is looking more attractive than I thought. I come away from her house feeling chirpy for once.

Be NICER to my mother
Note to cleaner

April 28th

YOUNGEST has been auditioned and given a part in the summer term production of *In the Mood*. Great excitement, until we are sent the rehearsal schedule which stretches throughout the summer term and into – can you imagine – the autumn term too. Twice a week. Better be bloody good. Except you know it won't be, it'll be 60 girls standing on stage all at once, trying to get a look-in with the usual three getting all the solos and the limelight.

To DO
Costume hire place
Shoe repairer's

April 30th

One of the wonderful things about being of a certain age is that on the whole it means I am excused dating; having been married to the same man for 18 years I have got rather out of practice. Not that when I was in practice I was any good at it in the first place, mind you. I could never read the signs accurately: either someone fancied me and thought he'd made it crystal clear over a period of six months and then years later admitted it and I had never noticed, or I fancied someone and made a

complete hash of trying to convey it. And I was completely
rubbish at dumping people and getting dumped. I would do
anything not to have to actually dump someone, avoid them,
pretend I was about to elope with his best friend, anything; and
then when people dumped me I didn't really get it, when they
said the euphemistic 'I think we are getting too serious', I was
stupid enough to take it literally, and suggest perhaps we should
see one another, then, less frequently. Dur . . . These days
people probably just do it on the text – 'u, dumped' or 'u fancy
one?' – dating must be a lot easier.

This newfound rush of libido is getting out of hand. I've
started to fancy all sorts of absurdly unsuitable and frankly
rather odd people. Went into Doug's Shoe Bar to get some shoes
heeled, and found myself rather fancying, well, Doug.
He's late fifties, little specs and wears shorts all year round. Nice
knees. Think I might need to see a counsellor.

May

May 1st

GRUMPY OLD MAN in a strop about us not having
any single cream for his beloved late-night Mr Kipling Bakewell
tarts. 'It's in the fridge.' 'It's not, I've looked.' 'It is definitely in
the fridge. Look properly.' What does he want, a grid reference?

To Do
Find Inland Revenue form
Put P45 in safe place

May 2nd

Unusually pleasant shopping trip to buy big new fridge with
GOM. Have been daydreaming about buying one for weeks –
especially during hideously pointless Powerpoint presentation
on Nurturing Change last week. Hideous waste of time that was.
Have always wanted fridge with ice crusher and cool-water

dispenser like they have in *Friends,* and am planning to buy some stainless-steel shiner from Lakeland to polish on weekly basis. Am salivating at the thought.

I don't often go shopping with GOM, but I notice he is so much more friendly to people than I am. Feel ashamed. He's especially friendly to people with young children, turning into a premature grandfather without the grandchildren, leaning into babies' prams and making mad Donald Duck impression noises and doing that thing with his fingers and cheeks saying 'pop goes the weasel'. It was fun when he was a young dad, when the girls were little and we went to playgroup, but now he's just a bit scary frankly, people look taken aback, and it's very ageing. Makes me feel older – being married to a trainee grandad . . . Wish there was a subtle way of telling the world that I'm probably still ovulating. I suppose I could buy some leather trousers.

To Do
Clear out old fridge
Buy citrus fridge freshener
Suss out leather trousers

May 3rd

Spring is finally here, bird table activity very brusque, have bought Ladybird book but so far only thing I can recognise is a robin, and that's because it has a red breast and you get them on Xmas cards. Have started to put my failed breadmaker loaves on it, but to date the birds haven't eaten any of them and there is a pile of loaves like house bricks, and about as heavy, on the table.

If it falls on someone's foot
there will be major mishap. It
looks a bit like a piece of
modern art. If I lived in
Islington I could sell it to the
Tate Modern and call it
something daft, make some
money. But have to admit
defeat and bin the loaves since
the birds – whatever make they
are – have ignored them.
Ungrateful wretches.

   The days are suddenly longer and sat
outside at lunchtime with Tupperware
(lockable obviously): cottage cheese, low-fat
coleslaw and raw carrot, since it is Monday and the diet has
started big time. Came back to desk and had toffee crisp from
machine, followed by usual self-loathing . . . but I feel so much
better having been outdoors, watching the trees with their new
leaves waving in the breeze. Am made happy by simple things
now I find. Got home and told the girls what lovely leaves I saw
at lunchtime, and they gave me that look – the one that means:
'You sad old cow who cares about the frigging leaves?'

   All this longing for fresh air and outdoor activity can only
lead to me being one of those mad old bats who swim in the
Serpentine or the North Sea every morning even in October.
I'm developing the body for it too.

To Do
Book holiday – camping?
Visit Tate Modern when in London next

May 4th

I've been looking forward to today for months. I am ashamed of myself. Utterly ashamed. That I feel this way about YOUNGEST's next appointment with the orthodontist.

State-of-the-art orthodontistry will guarantee that YOUNGEST emerges after 18 months with a set of teeth like Julia Roberts to go with her babestastic walk and skinny-winny hips and thighs. But in the meantime, while she is still in this chrysalis stage, she will have to wear a hideous brace. Or that's what I'm hoping. Let's be honest, it's going to make me look that bit better by comparison. Shocking, I know . . .

What did YOUNGEST do to deserve this? Apart from ruining my pelvic floor, giving me early onset stress incontinence and what she used to call my jelly belly. What she has done is turn me into my own mother. Now that she is approaching adulthood, she is making me come out with attitudes that my mother used to come out with when I was her age.

I've started putting my kitchen rubbish in old carrier bags rather than in the bin, like my mother does. I hoover on a Saturday morning when everyone is still in bed, like she did. I've not bought any extra strong mints yet. YET. But none of this was going to happen to me. I was going to be the very model of liberal, enlightened motherhood. I went to National Childbirth Trust classes. I drove a 2CV. But suddenly since YOUNGEST became the sneery teenager from hell, I've started to use my mother's vocabulary. 'I'm just popping out to the shops,' I say. 'Cheerio', 'Mind how you go' or 'Whoops a daisy'. It's all so middle-aged. So uncool.

The reception area in Orthodontics is very Early Learning Centre, and the walls are painted with a hideous multi-coloured mural probably painted by some work-experience kids with negligible talent, and a video of *Postman Pat* is playing in the corner. 'Oh this is nice, darling,' I say. Sarcasm escapes her still, but I enjoy it.

Conversation with her is a bit strained. As ever. And is naturally totally one-way. There isn't anything she would ever want to say to me. Except maybe to ask where I've put her hair gel, or to ask for pocket money . . . sorry, her allowance.

'Have you had a nice day at school, love? Much homework?'

'You asked me that in the car.'

'Oh, sorry.'

'What did you have for lunch?'

'Can't you think of anything more interesting to ask me?'

'What did you do in physics, then?'

'We don't *do* physics on Thursdays. Anyway it's just science. Not physics. We don't DO physics.'

'He's going to give me a brace like Veronica Bryce's, isn't he?'

'You don't know, darling. He might give you one to just put in at night.'

Sometimes I can be so two-faced.

'I think it's time we got these teeth straightened out, YOUNG LADY,' says the orthodontist. At least other people get it all wrong with her too. And there it is. The little beauty. Gleaming and sparkling under the lights. Like a piece of postmodern metallic sculpture. Looking as if it might double as a waste disposer if you plugged it in the mains.

YOUNGEST looks as if she might pass out. Or be sick. Or both. Then I go and feel sorry for her. Because prolonging her childhood is perhaps the real reason why I'm keen on the brace – a way of keeping her (and me) together in her childhood which seemed a safer place to be than her imminent adulthood.

She starts to sob again in the car and now the whole thing is ruined. I'd hoped to swan off and feel all excellent about this, and now she's made me feel sorry and protective. Sometimes motherhood is a tough old game.

TALK TO
GOM
about
upping
YOUNGEST'S
~~allowance~~
~~pocket~~
~~money~~
allowance

May 5th

The HRT is still having the effect of increasing my libido. The GRUMPY OLD MAN is going the other way, sooner be sorting his vinyl collection or writing to Radio 4. Spiteful of God to plan things this way. It's not exactly as though I can just go out and get some nookie of my own, like I might go out to the Garden Centre and get some climbing hydrangeas. Not without making a complete fool of myself. If you were some old fading celebrity, you'd have a toy boy, some squeaky clean young boy who held your hand at parties and then married you when you promised to give him a share of the loot. You can't tell me they'd be a good lay. They'd be after all your nice moisturisers in the bathroom. But someone who found me utterly urgently irresistible again would be jolly nice. I don't mean anything remotely complicated or too tiring. I can't be doing with anything romantic or emotionally demanding, it's more that I could fancy some good hard urgent sex – no questions asked. Wham bam, thank you, mam. So what's a girl to do?

Found myself thinking about the postman the other day when I answered the door in my dressing gown and had to sign for a parcel. As if I was in a Benny Hill sketch with the milkman. But, you know, I am ashamed to see how it can happen, how a woman of a certain age could go for someone like that. I don't want any emotional involvement or a silly affair, I just want the odd one-night stand. Probably with the lights off. With someone who looks a bit better than some saddo trainspotter with a personal hygiene problem who would be likely to pick me up if I

was sad enough to go and sit at a bar somewhere.

I don't want to lurk about in silly singles bars, or go speed dating . . . Strikes me that just plain being able to pay for it might be an idea. I mean buying the odd half-hour with the kind of bloke you'd have gone for in your twenties, or would have gone for you, more to the point. But where? It'd have to be somewhere totally respectable; obviously I couldn't be doing with going into massage parlours or red-light districts, but say it was somewhere like the Ideal Home exhibition, or John Lewis. It could be in Haberdashery, somewhere no one would suspect was anything other than the kind of place middle-aged invisible women go to hang out and choose knitting patterns or buttons. Even if you went with the GOM you could say it was a broderie anglaise demonstration, say you'd meet him at Asda in half an hour, he wouldn't know the difference. That way you could have some delicious young Adonises who might like to make a bit of money on the side. We could make sure it was nice and neat and tidy – half-hour sessions would be fine – and then we could get on. No one would be the wiser.

Of course in the unlikely event that I was on the pull, on the market, I'd have to buy some condoms. No getting away from it. Where from? Why can't they sell them at Lakeland, never mind the biscuit carrier or the microwave splatter shield, what about something to put in your handbag that looks like an apple corer or a portable pan scourer but comes with some condoms in a hidden compartment. Not like those stupid tampon holders that are supposed to look stylish and subtle in your bag but look like nothing else but tampon holders in turquoise, something clever.

You'd still have to buy them though. I know, better still . . . Lakeland should just put some in with the postage and packing, there should be a subtle box you can tick on the form which doesn't say condoms yes or no but something in code like, would you like your postage donated to hungry African elves, and you can tick it . . . and they know. Then when your bird-table tidy arrives and the condoms fall out you can tut and say, 'Goodness what do they do that for?' and then sneak a few away in a secret store.

Shocking, isn't it? It's just that people assume we don't want sex any more. Well, we do . . . and then again we don't. It's a bit all over the place, like everything else.

To DO
Cif mousse
Lakeland catalogue

May 6th

Join a telephone queue to mobile phone company to ask why I still have not had a refund for returned fancy mobile. We go through the usual five or six options and I wait for as long as it takes to hear the calming music loop at least twice, and then they come on and offer a new option. I jump to attention because I think with flush of excitement that I am about to get through to a person. Joy of joys! Alas, no, it announces that they are doing a survey on customer satisfaction with mobile services and that this survey will not affect your place in the queue and that it will take 15 seconds. Dilemma. If you spend the 15 seconds out of the queue, will it mean that you get fast-tracked because you have been teacher's pet, or is it a double bluff as it tempts losers like me to spend an extra 15 seconds and lose my place in the queue and they'll have my postcode and that'll mean more catalogues with Peruvian woollen socks on the hall floor?

So I go for it, out of desperation as much as anything else, and hey presto I get through fast as fast. Chirpy woman tells me her name is Rita, yes yes yes, like I care what her name is, like we're going to be new best friends, and she asks me a series of stupid multiple-choice questions: am I more satisfied or less satisfied, is it a 6 or a 7 score, 6 being the least satisfied, it's hard not to lose my temper but of course you play ball because you are still in the queue, or so they say. They do ask me for my postcode, which was the big one I was expecting, but in desperation I give it to her (if I had been thinking fast enough I would have given her someone else's – like Jocasta's or my mother-in-law's). And they pass you back to the main menu . . . Marvellous. Back to the chirpy music, but now there's a message saying you are . . . electronic pause . . . number 12 in the queue. Result. Only another eight minutes or so and you actually get through to someone who says they will look into it.

But there is fall-out like you would expect, and it's a lot worse than Peruvian knitwear catalogues; you are contacted on a weekly basis from now to establish whether you are now more or less satisfied with their service than you were when they conducted the telephone survey. And by other companies that have been passed your number. I could cheerfully lob my mobile into a bog. And it would give me great pleasure. But for only about two minutes and then it would be extremely annoying.

To DO
Wash front step
Put note in diary to check if refund
    comes through with next statement

May 10th

Wondrous new fridge delivered, like the one in the background on all the cookery TV shows. Spent the afternoon organising where I am going to keep everything.
Feel like Doris Day or Martha Stewart.
My life is complete. Well, it would be complete if it was plumbed in. They didn't mention that the thing needs a plumber to install it. Yes, right, so that's going to be easy, isn't it?

FIND
PLUMBER

May 15th

Call plumber.

May 16th

Call new plumber.

May 17th

Plumber arrives. I have to sign a form which confirms the exact time of his arrival. When I say his exact time of arrival, I mean he looks at his watch and asks me to check with mine, and he puts in a big box on the form – arrival time – 17.12. He charges £75 for the first hour and then £50 for anything into the next hour. In my next life I am going to be a plumber; even poking around in people's loos is worth it with this kind of money. He's probably going to retire at 35, already holidays at

Sandy Lane in Barbados with the Michael Winners of this world
. . . and I think of poor ELDEST studying for A level Classics,
Greek and French, why bother, makes me feel like suggesting
she just becomes a lady plumber, she'd clean up – but literally,
unfortunately.

I don't offer him a coffee, what with the meter running so
seriously. He hooks the back of the fridge up in less than five
minutes, so in a flush of gratitude I do make him a cup of coffee.
He chats to me, I feel like saying 'How much is this costing me?
If I didn't think you were so arrogant and objectionable I might
get my money's worth and suggest some hanky-panky upstairs,
kill two birds with one stone.' But by the time he is packing up it
is about 17.56. Suddenly I notice there is now a red light on by
the water dispenser. It's still not actually dispensing water. I
hand him the manual, like he can have the miserable job of
looking it up, but aware that I only have about 15 minutes left of
his meter running. He hands it back to me, disinterested,
unmoved – 'You have to contact stockists to get a water filter.' I
sign the out time with bad temper. Could easily have toddler
tantrum right here and now on the kitchen floor. If I really was a
toddler in this sort of mood someone would put me in the high
chair with the safety restraints.

I ring up the shop where we bought the wretched fridge,
go through two idiotic assistants before I can get to someone
with some sense and they say, 'You have to go on to the website.'
Go on to the website, so that's nice and convenient, isn't it?
Getting logged on and on to the website takes another 15
minutes. The whole thing seems to be based in Detroit and the
help section is something only teenagers can navigate through,
and naturally there is no phone number to ring. So I email them
in the little box 'contact us' and explain my problem as politely
as possible. Which is not very politely. Then I log on for the next

three days in the hope that someone has answered. I might have known this fridge was cheaper than the other ones for good reason.

These days everything in the kitchen seems to be a battleground. Our mothers were thrilled to bits with their new Formica, Bakelite and high-level grills – tickled pink with their new Kenwood mixer and Tupperware – but as usual we had to mess with it. Turn it into rocket science. Space shuttles have control panels that are easier to operate than your average kitchen these days. Every new appliance comes with another stupid booklet to clog up the drawer. The oven's complicated with knobs on. Hundreds of knobs. All devilishly pointless, 17 different ways to roast a chicken. Never mind reading the manual – you need to go on a course to use some of it. It's only a casserole, dear. We're not splitting the atom.

Even the microwave – designed with the slovenly in mind – has gone all fancy pants and multiple choice. What with plated meals and crispy tops and fast boil, the usual pointless palaver. Which is convenient for whom exactly?

Eventually Detroit fridge filter mission control replies saying I have to go to registered stockists of filters, which doesn't include the shop where I bought it, so I have to ring directory enquiries – a joy in itself. I go through a million options on the recorded menu and eventually leave a message. I could kill, I really could. The red light will still be on by Christmas, I know it.

To Do
Call Stockists about filter
Complain to shop where I bought fridge

To Do
Organise garden clear-up
Carpet cleaner for mud marks .

May 20th

Come home from work to find house in a chaotic mess, not because the kids have wrecked it but because GOM is off work using up his annual leave. He's had a massive onslaught on the garden. Which means that he has weeded but got bored with it, so borders that were perfectly OK are now a mess.

May 21st

Come down in the morning to find that kitchen is hideous blood-splattered murder scene. Dog looking sheepish in her bed and on further examination reveals remains of a dead bat. Bad enough, but in her excitement at chasing the bat around – presumably in the middle of the night – she has shat herself, which in addition to the blood everywhere on the walls, is a great start to the day. Having to get on your knees with some rubber gloves on to clean it all up and then bag it all up and take to the bin – and all before 7am.

To DO
Buy disposable rubber gloves
Bleach
Call about fridge filter

May 23rd

Now we have bats in the house. They are all over the place. I mean it's one thing to have them swooping around in the garden, but on the landing it's a bit much.

Watching *Desperate Housewives* last night, just minding my own business and one swooped right in my hair. Every time one appears, all three of us females in the house start screaming and covering our heads like we're in Alfred Hitchcock's *The Birds*. GOM caught one in a fishing net – could have kissed him I was so impressed. Had a look at it when it was captive in net and was shocked to see it had a face; I'm sure it winked at me. Had to call in the Bat Protection Society and a strange woman with shoes that looked like tractor tyres, long hair, patchwork hippy trousers and red satchel turned up. Apparently we are not allowed to get rid of them or even disturb them because they're a protected species so we have to live with them in the house, they could be swarming for months . . . Far from realising how we are all under house arrest, afraid to open any door in case one or two of them come swooping out at us like the Red Arrows, she seemed quite envious. She probably goes to Glastonbury.

TO ~~DO~~

Call about fridge filter
Get hobby

May 30th

I have developed a bit of an obsession about the family next door. 'Happy Family' I call them. Since they moved in I've taken to looking into their kitchen more than is probably good for me (the kitchen is the only easily visible room unless I stand at the bottom of the garden where I can see directly into their living room, but a woman of my age who snoops into other people's houses easily turns into Hilda Ogden and it would not be good for my image at all). She is in her early thirties, with long dark hair that she plonks up in one of those plastic bulldog clips – very good-looking in a motherly I've-been-out-for-some-fresh-air sort of way. She's a stay-at-home mum as far as I can see, and husband is dark, very good-looking and smiles and laughs a lot. They are obviously blissfully happy and I have even seen them dancing in the kitchen. When do we ever do anything as joyous as that?

The bit of the kitchen in my viewfinder extends from the sink backwards to the kitchen table (half of) and the noticeboard behind. You can tell an awful lot about a family from this particular slice of their environment. Or I can. I never see any takeaway cartons stacked up on the draining board, and there is endless evidence of creative play for the children. Lots of gorgeous kids' drawings and things made out of paper plates and plaster of Paris stuck on the noticeboard or on the kitchen table for all to admire for weeks on end. Home-made bread on cooling racks. She has a sewing machine that I can sometimes see half of on the kitchen table – curtains, girls' dresses, all sorts of gorgeous home-making activities that make me feel profoundly useless. The kids look untidy but cheerful, and are often cuddled up with Mum or Dad over a bowl of hot chocolate or a good book. Sometimes I think I'm peering into this kitchen just in order to find something wrong, some evidence of unhappiness or dysfunction that would make me feel better. I never find it. Today in their kitchen is something that looks like home-made Father's Day cards and on the drying-up rack are four bowls and a soup ladle – probably the aftermath of some organic wholesome home-made soup. I was never that good a mother. Makes me sick.

Go to beautician for usual waxing ritual, bikini line has become a spreading mass of hair. Once it was really only just around the line of my pants, now just as it's all thinning round my front bottom it's on the move, all growing rapidly like a lot of ground elder towards my knees. Spiteful beautician says it was really now more of an upper leg and lower leg wax than the usual half leg and bikini job. Would have argued with her if she had not been on the action end of the waxing strips in what I can only describe as an excruciating area. She also suggests a non-interventionist facial, which effectively is getting yourself plugged into a load of electrodes and pulling faces to tauten and tighten up your facial muscles which in my case are – I notice with horror – starting to sag. All very depressing. Then, cheek of it, she says would I like her to deal with some of the blackheads. If only I had known being a beautician would have meant such a thing I wouldn't have bothered going to university at all. The idea of earning a living popping other people's blackheads would have been all the job satisfaction needed.

Home, and I am in the pyjamas and slippers in a jiffy. I think when I get into my dressing gown of an evening I actually make a kind of sighing noise like the one my mother makes when she takes her first sip of tea.

The usual rollercoaster of moods. One minute I am relaxed and content with the world, next I am in a filthy black mood, and all it took was switching on the telly and seeing *America's Top Model*.

To DO
Find receipt for fridge and Trading
                Standards address
First class stamps

June

June 1st

It's the first anniversary of my father's death, and we don't really know what to do as a family to mark it. There is no headstone or memorial statue or roundabout or road named after him, so we cling together, me and my mother, and are in a sobby mess most of the day, torturing ourselves looking at his diary during the last few weeks before his death. He hadn't written a lot, most of it a string of specialist and doctor's appointments, but on the last week he wrote in wobbly writing 'I love you all' and on the last day but one he wrote 'Abide with me', which was his way of saying he wanted that hymn played at his funeral. And I wish we had it on tape or we could go to church and ask for it to be played or something. Death seems such an awkward occasion to mark and of course that's partly because we have allowed all the traditions and church to drop away from our

HOT FLUSH AGAIN

lives. We go to the Abbey and light a candle and sob some more. You only get one Mum and one Dad and it's only when they're going, or gone, that you realise just how precious they are.

To Do
Sort out photo albums
Take Mother out more
Pick up prescription

June 2nd

Read an article on IT information about how much your boss knows about you. It's bad enough she knows I am rubbish at writing reports and leave early on Thursdays but apparently on top of knowing all about your emails, bosses can tell exactly how much time you spent logged on to which websites. Better stop shopping on-line at Tesco's and Lakeland. Worse than that, apparently all the emails you delete get copied into a special top-secret deleted file for your boss to see – so all those emails you don't want anyone to know about are picked out for special attention. Like for instance the ones you sent to chum in Manchester office about how much you detested your opposite number in Glasgow, or the one you sent to ex-boyfriend arranging lunch or – by far the worst – the ones you sent about Jocasta saying, 'Have you seen what Jocasta is wearing today? I can see her bra. Get a room . . .' Those are the ones that automatically get saved to a file and presumably are put in front of your boss quite succinctly in a manageable and rather interesting beginning of the day ritual. Am viewing her with new eyes. Will need to watch this. And plan to delete every email I send immediately so she is inundated with deleted data from my email address – that way she will get bored with it v. quickly. Mind you, she doesn't look that busy at the moment.

To Do
Set up Yahoo email account
Delete some deleted emails

June 4th

We're all dashing about cramming a month's work into one day, so if there's one thing that gets us madder than anything else it's someone holding us up for a second or two. Which means that the whole business of daily life is more stressy than most of us can cope with. AND the icing on the cake is that someone – probably a civil servant – spends their day thinking up 100 NEW ways to hold us up or catch us out, or dreams up a spitefully confusing set of speed regulations or parking rules that you'd have to be a member of Mensa to figure out. No waiting, maximum three hours, Monday to Thursday 8am to 9.30, what? Can I park there or can't I? Speak in plain English please. Then there's all the pay and display nonsense. Fiddling about with coins and stickers that you can't get off afterwards. Why can't we have free valet parking for all, like they do apparently in Hollywood. That's what I call a party manifesto. Want the female vote, you can start with that. Failing that, put a grumpy old woman in charge. Have it sorted in a jiffy.

It's all so tiresome and tedious . . . half the time you can't even park outside your own house. I mean I don't even live in central

London, so I don't think that's too much to ask. It's tempting to put your own traffic cones out. Suddenly I am drawn to one of those stupid signs people put outside their house, on their garden wall, which I always thought were tragic, NO PARKING or KEEP CLEAR AT ALL TIMES, the ones you see and immediately know are the work of some mad old Neighbourhood Watch warden or mad old bat, not by anyone official or important. The ones that when you were younger you ignored, or specifically parked in front of on purpose to annoy them.

If it's not stupid parking rules that hold you up it's the senseless series of holes in the road that are dug and then filled in again over and over and over again. They have to be doing that on purpose to annoy you too. Complained to woman from Happy Family next door about road being dug up again and stupid traffic-flow arrangements and she said hadn't really noticed, looked at me pityingly, like I am mad. Is there no end to her happy serene disposition? What is she on? Think I might go through her dustbins to find out.

To DO
Bottle bank
Pay parking fine

June 10th

The A level exams are in full swing . . . along with the inevitable heatwave. Endless glorious sunny days with temptingly blue skies just as my poor babies have to be sitting in exam halls.

To Do
Make home-made ice cream
Buy cracked heel cream
Review summer wardrobe.
Let out peasant skirt

June 12th

The annual travelling fair is in town. When I was young I used to worry about the odd thing, like whether Melanie Smith would get off with Graham Bostock, or how to get a tampon in, but on the whole life was a doddle. Now I could worry for a living. I could worry about everything and anything because the whole world is programmed to make me worry more, and when the fair comes to town my worry reaches its annual peak.

Curiously when I was a teeny-bopper I sought out scary things, scary was fun, scary was actually the point. Why else would you have gone to fairgrounds? OK so you might have wanted to know what a love bite was . . . But it was thrilling. You were excited. Now fairgrounds are my worst nightmare. Once a year the kids drag me off to a horrible muddy field with rides that are so dangerous you have to be strapped in like an astronaut. Rides have got bigger and bigger and bigger. The bigger, the higher, the more the kids want to go on it. I can't even watch. Not even bribing them with more pocket money is going to put them off. Worse, they want me to go on some too. Maybe I could start off with the dodgems . . . Except even they look really scary . . . there aren't any lanes, or lights, or helmets or safety belts. Maybe I could hog the outside lane, hog the edge and try to avoid everyone else – which is kind of missing the point.

The little kids' rides then. I could offer to look after someone's teeny-weeny. Could risk a little teacup – as long as no one pushes it too fast. Only one I dared to try was the trusty old-fashioned helter-skelter. The girls came on to humour me . . . Got halfway up and thought they must be infinitely bigger and taller than when I used to go on them as a kid, and had to come down step by step backwards and got myself clogged up and in a mess with upcoming toddlers. Help had to be sought.

Everything feels like the worst-case scenario. The rides run by a man who looks distracted and is more interested in page 3 of the *Sun*; it's making you so nervous you feel sick, you could throw up. In your mind the whole thing could so easily change from a harmless sunny carefree day at the fair to a massive disaster, tens of people crushed inside the machinery. Trouble is that no one else worries properly, not as properly as I do. Which means I have to be worrying for everyone else too. The whole world has to be worried for by me. No wonder I'm worn out.

To DO
Make home-made ice cream
Camomile tea

June 14th

At work I was in a particularly dreadful meeting today and found myself daydreaming about retiring, for the first time. When I was in my thirties retirement seemed so far off it was an impossibility. Tied in with pebble-dashed bungalows and scrimping and saving, saving margarine pots to grow seeds in and generally being on the scrap heap. Now the idea of planting little things in margarine pots and being able to listen to a play on Radio 4 in the afternoon seems like it could be fun. Well, fun is the wrong word – I don't really do fun any more – but I can imagine myself doing all that and feeling rather at peace somehow, relaxed, chilled, together. Although those afternoon plays on Radio 4 can be a bit rubbish, especially when they involve someone pretending to be American, which is alarmingly frequent . . . Someone who can't do an American accent to save their life. Evidently my grumpiness would be unlikely to evaporate. It's why people of my age suddenly start reading the financial pages. Suddenly they wake up to the fact that they need to save enough money to retire. It's taken me until middle age to realise that money is as important as it is in terms of giving us choice. I don't mean masses of money, I mean enough money to be able to make some lifestyle choices once in a while like, hey, I've been doing this job for 20 years now and do you know I would really rather like to spend some more time doing not very much. Might have the odd day without a 'to do' list. Now I really am entering the realms of fantasy.

TO DO
Find ice cream recipe
Call Citizens Advice Bureau —
*   find out about SIPP funds*

June 20th

Big programme on telly last night about woman with breast cancer. Sobbed uncontrollably, and so when I got out of the shower I took a look in the mirror and did a bit of checking for lumps. Nothing nearly as systematic as you should, but better than nothing . . . I put my bra on and I notice my skin is bulging under my armpit – there is a little pushy-out sort of lump that bulges over my bra. Am so shocked that adrenalin starts pumping round my body so much I have to go for a poo. Still in my dressing gown I get the book out. Find well-thumbed breast cancer page . . . One of the things you should look out for is a different shape of breast, some lump or pucker or bulge that is not normally there. Sweaty palms now. Am writing mental letters to the girls, thinking through what I should do first, go to India, resign in an attention-seeking flurry, make a speech in the middle of the office perhaps, send a moving email that is tragically emotionally charged.

Call the doctor's surgery and they say there is nothing till Thursday week. I pull out my trump card: 'I have found a lump.' You can hear in her voice that she has been taught to put people like me straight in, straight to the top of the list. Feel absurdly pleased with myself. '1.30 this afternoon.' I feel like air punching, I beat the system, got up the queue! The euphoria dies down when I remember why.

Spend the morning at work unable to do anything constructive but Googling 'breast cancer'. And look out my pension plan and prices of flights to India just in case I don't have time later. It's not that I actually positively think I am dying – yet – it's more that I am mentally preparing myself for the fact that one day I will, which of course is irrefutable and so might as well get some of the stuff done now. It doesn't help that every five minutes someone writes another book about all the things we are supposed to do before we die, or things we are supposed to see or the things we are supposed to say... It all makes me feel restless and even more stressed than usual. Endless books and TV programmes which only add to our 'to do' list, because most of us are too damn busy to get round to it. And I seem to have spent my whole time as a mother basically worrying about whether I am going to die, or the kids are going to die. When ELDEST was born, the stakes suddenly felt higher than I could possibly have imagined. I had to say to myself, if only she lives until her first birthday, her first party dress with a sash on the back, her first day at school, her first length at the swimming pool, if only I can live until she leaves school, until she goes to university – her very existence was so precious.

It's not entirely because I am neurotic, it's partly because I have experienced death in the family at first hand, and of course until you have you don't really have a handle on it. My father was one of my favourite people and I was the one to receive the news, the one called into the specialist's office; my mother was too scared. I remember walking in and doing my touch my collar, touch my toes little superstition routine, and saying to the specialist something jaunty when I went in like 'hope it's not going to be dreadful news', and him not correcting me, so then I knew, and then the Macmillan nurse came in . . . You know it's not going to be good news when they show up. My father only

had a very short time to live, they didn't say how long, but
suddenly, life was measured in a cup I couldn't get the measure
of and neither could he. There is never a good time to die. Never
a time when you think oh well, it's a fair cop. Life is simply
something everyone clings to.

I get into the doctor's surgery with my breast lump worry, and
blurt it out, and with it come tears. She examines my breasts
and gives me the strange all-over circling, stroking thing with
her hands and I have to concentrate very hard not to think about
the sexual connotations, concentrate on not giving her eye
contact while she is doing it, and trying not to let my nipples go
hard. And then she says, 'Where is this lump?' I sit up and say
well my skin is bulging, look under my left arm there's a little
pleat. I assume she is going to say, 'Oh yes, you're right, let's
whisk you straight into hospital, and by the way have you
thought of burial at sea, I hear it's all the rage,' but she makes
me stand up and put my bra on. Says, 'Have you thought of
getting a bra fitted in M & S?' 'What do you mean, a special bra?'
'No, just a bigger bra. The skin is pushing on both sides, you
need a bigger bra cup.'

I could kill her. As I'm getting dressed she puts the knife in
and says, 'Next time can we assume it's something ordinary?'

TO DO
Bra fitting appointment
Make home made ice cream
Buy write-your-own-will and testament
                    forms from Smiths
Throw out old bras
Get hobby

June 24th

YOUNGEST comes home with project work to do with musical production, which involves going to museum, making a gangster costume for her and for one chorus member, and a suggestion for private singing lessons with local tutor. Great, that's about a week's work then. Thanks for that.

To Do

Ring sewing woman down the road

June 26th

Glued a drawer back together as fed up with waiting for GOM to get round to it on his list of little jobs I have given him . . . and in any case likely as not if he does do it, it will come apart again. So I got the super glue out. Left it for five minutes in the pantry to set to find it had and, hey, what do you know, it has already come unstuck. Like it always does, unless presumably you stand there for 40 minutes holding it together with your fingers, in which case you would have successfully glued your fingers to the drawer as well. I just wish glue would work. Just the once would be nice.

JOBS FOR GOM
CREOSOTE FENCE
OIL BACK DOOR
WONKY WHEEL
(on wheelbarrow)
(FIND LIST I GAVE
GOM LAST CHRISTMAS)

June 27th

What is it with phrases and sayings? When you get older you are more prone to things getting on your nerves – it just happens, and the things people say generally set you off. And once you've noticed something that is annoying there is really no going back. Phrases such as 'no problem at all' when you ask for a coffee at Starbucks, well I didn't think there would be a problem – what with it being a café. I have started to say 'you take care'. People say, 'Gosh what a great idea, do you know I think I will from now on.' And one that just bugs me and I fear I will pass on to you once you realise, the phrase 'PIN number'; surely 'PIN' means 'personal identification number', so it's just a PIN not a PIN number. And breathe . . .

Happy Family house next door is for sale. Must be moving.

To Do
Buy ice cream
Find odd-job man

July

July 1st

Instigated brilliant new system in kitchen, which feels like the domestic equivalent of discovering penicillin. My brilliant new system is a solution to a daily problem, namely that no one knows in our house whether the dog and cats have been fed because there is no specific rota for who is responsible for feeding them. And we all end up having to text, phone, call up the stairs or down the garden to find out whether the animals have or haven't been fed at any one sitting, which is very annoying indeed. So I had a fantastic idea . . . I have typed out a big neat sign to keep by mission control next to the kitchen phone, which says ANIMALS ARE FED. This way the first person down in the morning (by person I normally mean adult, the children don't even think about feeding their pets) feeds all three animals and then props the sign up leaning on windowsill by the phone, thus avoiding overfed or underfed pets. Brilliant. So brilliant that I popped into the stationer's in town and had the sign laminated. Crikey, my whole life suddenly felt SORTED!

Inevitably I started to get carried away
. . . I might laminate some signs for upstairs too. Like one to say
the *immersion is on*, or one that says *lights* and *darks* for linen
basket. Then – alas – GOM points out big problem . . . the bubble
bursts . . . because the animals all need feeding twice a day, so
now the sign is propped up by the phone saying animals are fed,
but if it is still there at 4pm does that mean they have been fed a
second time, or just that no one has turned the sign back over
again? There is a dangerous period between feeds, and between
the sign being turned back down again and being put back up
again, where system breaks down. Because, come four o'clock in
the afternoon, whose responsibility is it to turn it back round the
other way so that we know at teatime that the animals have in
fact NOT been fed at all? Just as I start to feel my life is in order
and I am in control, the whole thing falls apart again. Of course I
could make two different laminated signs, one which said
animals fed am and the other which said animals fed pm – even I
can see that this is verging on dysfunctional behaviour, actually
never mind the verging on . . . People would come and see the
signs and think I needed help rather than want some signs of
their own.

I decide to stick with the one original sign and now there are
no phone calls from home in the morning about whether I have
fed the animals, but still phone calls in the afternoon. Have you
fed the animals? No, have you? In short, we are no further on,
plus we only got the pets in the first place for the children, and
we shall be joining the grumpy band of middle-aged empty
nesters who walk the dog, feed the cat and take the hamster to
the vet long after their darling children leave home. It's the
empty nester equivalent of being left holding the baby, or the
Labrador or the poodle or the gerbil. Only babies are interesting.

TO DO
Buy big bag of dog food
WORM DOG
Deet spray
Look into malaria melodrome tabs
  on internet and call Tropical Diseases
            Hospital in London

July 2nd

A small ad saying MYSTERY SHOPPERS WANTED caught my
eye – a large retail chain is looking for people to be mystery
shoppers to record on hidden camera the service their staff are
giving. Sort of restaurant inspectors but for shop staff. This job
has my name on it, I could do it standing on my head, and I
could certainly do it for a living. I ring the number to find out
more about it, but answer machine is bleeping that it's full.
Other people, eager to wreak their revenge, got there before me.
Damn!

Bumped into Happy Family Yummy Mummy next door.
They're not moving house, they're divorcing.

TO DO
Find out address of M & S head office
Throw away hippy skirt

July 3rd

It is a known fact that nothing gets done properly in our house unless I do it. Not homework, not cleaning, not ironing, not chores, not wiping work surfaces, not errands, messages . . . No one else remembers to clean the swing bin in the bathroom or empty the recycle container of old newspapers or clear up after themselves *properly*. GOM will do things his way, which is code for *not properly*. He will clear up in the kitchen, often to his favourite Del Shannon track, splashing the water all over the floor and doing a lot of putting in to soak, but the floor will not be swept, and the kitchen table not wiped. How much longer would it take him to do that? Trouble is when I complain about it I sound just like – you know who – my mother, or a bossy form captain or the teacher from hell. I can hear myself practically saying, how many times have I asked him to do that nicely. Properly. But I just sound like a headmistress. What's a girl to do, except give him plenty of what my mother would have called 'Little Jobs' to occupy him usefully, tasks which surely a man of his age is supposed to do, like washing the car and mending the plate rack, bleeding radiators, or mending a stopcock. But even this sort of thing takes a lot of chivvying to get done, a lot of 'when are you going to do it?'

To Do
Organic compost
Rucksack for ELDEST's trip
Visa for Ghana

July 5th

Still no holiday booked and so I took action. Asked YOUNGEST what she would really like to do with me and Dad – now that ELDEST isn't coming with us and we can't persuade any of her friends to come away with us. She barely looked up from *Big Brother,* which she is depressingly glued to, but said she wouldn't mind doing something exciting like Melanie's Mum and dad do, like mountaineering or canoeing: 'It's so boring going on holiday with you and Dad otherwise.'

To Do
Send off activity holiday brochures

July 6th

Look into ELDEST's room and feel sick with fear. She will only be living at home full time for another two weeks, then she's off to the other side of the world, somewhere so foreign, so alien, they don't even get *Neighbours*, enough said . . . In two weeks she begins her big adventure and then the biggest adventure of all, goes to university. I can't think where her childhood went, it just flew by in a big blurry flash, and now she is about to leave. And I could sob and sob and sob my heart out and then sob some more but she wouldn't understand for a second, why should she, how could she?

At the moment her room is a mess, it smells of perfume, and sweaty feet and drinking chocolate. Her bed's not made, the bin's overflowing, and her hair straighteners have been left on by accident, there are some of her sister's trousers under the

bed, rancid milk in cereal bowls and piles of *Heat* magazines. I
gaze at it, taking it all in, knowing that when she is gone the
room will be pristine tidy, bed made, bin emptied, cupboards
sorted because I shall want to spend time in here, and shall
prepare her room and her house for her return visits, whenever
and however frequent they are. I shall be left walking the dog
and sending her tragic emails about the cat and her sister's
gerbil, and telling her news from our neighbours about what
Jessica down the road is doing in Australia, and about the article
I saw in the *Courant* about one of her school friends getting
married on a beach in the Dominican Republic.

I look back at all those days of her childhood that I spent out
at the office, all those weeks when she was tiny, into *Rosie and
Jim*, into nursery rhymes, coming home from school with her
projects, I always had emails to check, faxes to send, calls to make.

'Why can't you come in to school on Wednesdays like Jake's
mum?' she'd ask. 'Because Mummy has to go to work.' But the
truth is Mummy didn't have to go to work, Mummy chose to go
to work, to spend days at conferences and working late. Coming
home with spreadsheets and what for. Now she is grown up and
soon she'll be gone. Little Rabbit, her favourite soft toy, is still
here, battered and old and still smelling of her childhood, when
I could have had all of her I wanted, when she held my hand as
we walked down the street, before I started to irritate her, and
soon she will be gone, and it is too late and there is no going
back. Need to get a grip.

The thing is my generation felt we should have careers, we
went to grammar school, we were the first generation of women
to be liberated, equal, the world was spread out in front of us,
we were encouraged to go far, to excel, to be brilliant, to
contribute. Not for us the role models of today like Coleen
McLoughlin or Posh Spice, our heroes were Germaine Greer,

Joan Baez, Laura Ashley, Mary Quant, women who did
something with their lives, had something to say. We had talks
about Albert Schweitzer in assembly, we had morals instilled
into us. We went to university, we did well, we did really well,
and when we became mothers we were expected to manage
both at once. We didn't feel we had the choice to be stay-at-
home mothers. We were told we could have everything. So we
tried to have everything, and look where it got us – into a
stressed-out mess mostly. Then inevitably our salaries were
pivotal to the family budget and we got mortgages, so what
financial choice did we have in the end?

Now things have turned upside-down again, stay-at-home
mothers seem to have the upper hand, standing around outside
the school gates in their Yummy Mummy tracksuits, ready to go
straight to the gym. In a sense they did what our mothers did:
married men who would provide for them, and stayed at home,
did lunch with their friends, did whatever the equivalent is of
coffee mornings, probably joined a book club, did their hair, had
time to be at home to make tea for the kids. To make matters
worse for the working mothers, in my experience these stay-at-
home mothers are the ones that cut corners, buy ready meals
and shop in M & S, and ironically it's the working mothers
racked with guilt that sweat over some home-made risotto or
cheese soufflés, otherwise they feel more of a failure than
before. If that were possible!

TO DO
Get hobby for me and YOUNGEST to do
        together – pottery classes?
Sort out family albums
Ask about mobile reception in Ghana

July 19th

The night before ELDEST goes off to Ghana we get the map out, she shows where she's going and it hits home – she is going to the other side of the world without us, and it will be the first of many times I have no doubt; how on earth do people manage whose children emigrate to Australia? Now when I meet such women I'll talk to them knowing a little of their agony, the agony of not seeing enough of their kids. Even when their kids are 30 or 40 or 50, and I don't suppose it ever gets easier.

To DO
Set alarm to make cooked breakfast
for ELDEST

July 20th

We drive ELDEST to Heathrow; I feel sick. She has the largest rucksack I have ever seen, poor love is going to have to carry it – she's on her first long-haul flight without us, not even any of the others in the party are there to travel with – she's on a different flight from them. It feels like I might never see her again – and the enormity of it all in my mind and in my heart is so much bigger and rawer than I had anticipated . . . I manage to keep up a front until we get to the bit where you say goodbye and they go into security, the bit that's partitioned off so you can't see them for long. She hugs Dad, she hugs me, and I say I love her so much and cry. There are other people crying too – it's like it says in that wonderful film *Love Actually*, it's here you can see love up close. People saying goodbye – and here hopefully in two months' time where we will say hello again, to a girl who will

have changed, inevitably, a girl who will probably be blotchy red
with sunburn, mossie bites and probably skinnier, more mature,
more grown up. I look forward to it already . . . but I look at her
as she walks away knowing that the girl is now gone for ever,
and a young woman will return. Actually I think GOM cries a bit
too. Feel like hanging about on the edge of the airport perimeter
with all those mad plane spotters to see the plane go off, catch a
last glimpse of her being part of my world, but that would be
both stupid and prolonging the agony. I can visualise her
excitement, think of myself at her age and think how excited I
would have been to get on a plane without my parents, without
the world knowing who I was, incognito, with my life in front of
me, my exams done, my childhood over.

Can't even pull myself together. Come home and decide not to
change her bed. When GOM is snoring I will be able to use it as a
refuge and like a lovesick girlfriend think I will sleep in it and
smell her smell, feel like I am near her again. Need to pull myself
together. Spend the rest of the day moping like lovesick teenager.
I wonder whether I could log on and get weather forecast for
Ghana; Google name of village on her itinerary and nothing
comes up. Maybe I could call *National Geographic*, or the
meteorological office to keep an eye on any major weather
disasters or fronts that might be on the way, text her in time to get
out of the area; buy myself time once or twice a week on a satellite
dish that floats over the region where she'll be teaching to keep
check. As if I was Jack Bauer in 24. Well, it might be possible.

TO DO
Call gap organisers
Buy airmail stamps
Call ELDEST's best friend –
                    has she got a text?

July 21st

Haven't heard from her.

My mother calls round with a load of forms and letters from the building society saying she can't understand what she has to do with them, if anything, can I help. My father used to do all this for her, now guess what, I have to. You lose one child and in effect gain another.

July 22nd

View YOUNGEST with new eyes. Try to savour her presence knowing that when she goes it will be even worse, being the last one gone and then the nest will be well and truly empty, which will be doubly hard. But in some ways ELDEST going brings YOUNGEST and me closer together, and GOM and me too. We are all coming to terms with the same thing and we subconsciously savour one another the more because of it. But I still wish she was here and not in Ghana.

To DO
Post parcel to Ghana

July 23rd

Torture myself looking at some photos of ELDEST and of the four of us together. It makes me think of my father's disappearance act. By which I mean him dying. I remember I went into the room where he died downstairs soon after they took him away in the big blue van, the one all polished and clean that you know has got dead bodies in once you've seen one, looking under the bed the next day as though he was just hiding under it, not dead at all. Silly. Stupid. But how can someone as wonderful, as important, as significant to me have disappeared into thin air? Get a grip, I know rationally it's not the same, obviously, please God it isn't, but I feel like I am trying to come to terms with something similar. Know that when I look at the stars over the next eight weeks I will think of her, think of whether she will be looking at the same stars that night, or whether they look different where she is, like I look at the stars with my father dead and wonder if he is among them, which naturally he is, because I look up at them and think of him, which amounts to the same thing.

To Do
Call gap organisers
Check my emails are working

July 24th

At last a text from ELDEST saying 'Hey! Having great time. Village is cool. X'

A kiss – I don't remember a text of hers ever having a kiss on the end.

Saw *The Constant Gardener* about a woman murdered in deepest Africa. Wish I hadn't – it was like watching *Titanic* on a cruise ship. Life is cheap in the third world. My daughter's is very precious indeed. Am getting melodramatic. Don't care. Shall if I want to.

Came home to find email from ELDEST's best friend to say she had a text saying she is having a wonderful time and was dancing to reggae on the beach on Saturday. Will have to stop worrying, I can't worry about her for eight weeks solid, although it feels like if I do carry on worrying and am constantly vigilant, that in some way the worrying will help to keep her safe, which is obviously nonsense. But I shall try to scale down the worry a little.

To DO
BUY GUARDIAN
Ask her best friend to ask her to text
        to say she is OK and to be
    careful of the sea – rip tides etc.

July 25th

My birthday. Without her. But she left a card. Cling to it like a stupid woman who should know better. Keep it in my bag – and will do for months.

To DO
ASK Mother-in-law for receipt for silk
    scarf she sent me for my birthday

July 26th

I never read the foreign news or international pages in the paper – as I have got older I've got much worse at this – read all the girly bits like the gossip, and the telly pages, perhaps fuel my anxiety with a national disaster or personal tragedy story, something with photos, easy to read. But since Ghana has come on to my radar I am reading the foreign pages every day, mostly looking for articles about Africa. People at work look impressed.

To Do
Check Foreign Office website for
                politically unstable regimes

July 27th

Dog has developed big lump on her gums. No choice but to go to the vet's. To my dismay vet says dog has got serious dental work to be done, as in crowns, fillings, root canal work, and I must clean and floss her teeth daily from now on. I think I looked appalled, shocked and revolted all at the same time. If you think I am going to floss a dog's teeth even once, never mind every day, you have another think coming. I'm already having to shave off my mother's corn, which is bad enough, so I am sure as hell not flossing the dog's teeth. He says he will send a quote for the dental work, would I be after the porcelain with gold, or just the metal ones? I think you know the answer.

To DO
Dog bad-breath tablets
Book dental check up for me
                and youngest

July 28th

The letter arrives with quote for dog's dental work and it comes to nearly £500. Don't think I am going to tell YOUNGEST. I wouldn't even spend that on my own teeth. The world has gone mad.

Go to shoe shop to buy summer sandals at lunchtime to cheer myself up. Women like buying shoes – it is a given known fact. Well, they like shoes that's true. But shoe shops are a special sort of hell. I am now simply incapable of wearing very high heels, not only do they give me backache, but because I'm getting a bit beefy, a bit bigger all over, I look like Les Dawson. The whole world is in stilettos. People walk around in absurd gold things for evening that if I wore them I would simply have to hold on to something or someone all evening; try to go to the loo and I would need crutches or a calliper, and the dance floor would be out of the question. I look like a bad transvestite in heels, or a giant poodle. They simply make me look ridiculous. These days the omnipresent, omnipotent Trinny and Susannah makes us all wear high heels at all times; even to fill the car up with petrol, even with a pair of jeans, now you have to wear heels – it is compulsory, it is the law.

The girl takes ages to even come over, despite my pushy sarky expression (which obviously means in fact that rather than rushing to my aid, she makes me suffer, comes to me last after everyone else). 'Can you get me this in a size 7 ½?' I say. 'We don't do half-sizes, madam.' She says the word 'madam' with a bit of attitude. 'Then in 7 and 8 please.' I know she is going to be ages and ages and ages, probably nip out once she's gone through that silly swing door and go and have her Cornish pasty, text some friends, nip out to the bank and then come back and still say she hasn't got any in my size. Cow. Either that or she's going to linger about while I try them on and lie to me about how good they look to get me to buy the ones that will make me look most ridiculous.

When she does eventually come back with them they all look absurd and are either ridiculously uncomfortable or make me look like a district nurse. What is a woman to do? Hasn't cheered me up at all. I throw them all down in a childish fit of temper and go back to work without shoes. Having wasted a good 40 minutes.

To DO
Send off for shoes from catalogue
Ghanaian website –
        do they get tornadoes?

July 30th

ELDEST has been away only 10 days, still 33 to go. Missing her badly.

August

August 1st

The thing about gardening is that it seems like a great idea until you get out in the garden and start gardening, and then it seems like a lousy stupid idea. I get home and it's a gorgeous evening, and think there would be nothing nicer than getting the wheelbarrow out and the secateurs and the kneely thing someone bought me for my birthday, and off I go, creating little piles of weeds and clumps of soil, and a large wheelbarrow full of branches, and then my back starts to get a bit sore and my knees get a bit stiff, and I realise that I have only weeded and tidied about a 400th of the whole garden and I am cream-crackered. Picking things up off the kitchen floor when I drop them is at my age tedious enough, but at least accidental; this is self-imposed inconvenience and discomfort. Suddenly it feels spookily like housework but outdoors, with the added complication of where to put all the stuff once you've weeded it and trimmed it back and yanked it out of the soil? You sure as hell can't put it in the dustbin, dustmen being what they are, and to go to the tip you are going to have to put it in bags and get soil in your car, great. It's like having a good spring clean in the house and having to bag up all the dirt you collect and find a home for it.

I like my garden, yes, but the truth is that I like *sitting* in my garden, I like lolling in it on the (very) rare occasions it is warm enough to do so, and so gardening itself is perhaps not really as enjoyable as I think it is. I could do with zenning the whole thing, taking a weapon of mass destruction to the lawn, borders, everything, until nothing green is left, then gravel it, with some neat huge stone pebbles in a row and some concrete lolling areas and the ubiquitous water feature. Zero maintenance, zero faff, zero grump . . . It might look a touch like the local crematorium, or a high-security exercise block, but I would be able to loll every minute the sun was out. Perhaps I am losing it.

To DO
Weedkiller
Big bags
Get wheelbarrow mended – wheel loose

August 2nd

I don't know why it's taken me so long to get into the Suma catalogue. My friend Sarah and the other women in her street of a striped-jumper-and-organic-cauliflower disposition swear by it, have a kind of street co-operative whereby they all order in bulk and then distribute it, which is both marvellously cheap and environmentally friendly. They all buy organic couscous or Mexican bean soup, and ecologically sound loo cleaner, and Suma deliver to the door. So, sucked in to this heady solution to having one or two things ticked off the list, along I go. They only do orders in vast numbers, which means people have to group together to pour over the catalogue and tick it all off on tragic order forms together. There are precious few photos of what you're buying. Someone acts as head girl and then divides it all up in their garage – so the process takes a good evening.

Naturally, when the order eventually comes everyone staggers home with a boot load of stuff. I get home and find I have a sack the size of a pillow of oats, 24 cans of mung beans in brine, 36 tins of organic mango chunks and six litres of organic cranberry juice. What seemed like such an economic and ecologically sound grocery order is now doing three (bad) things: it's clogging up my kitchen cupboards, overspilling into the garage and spare room, and it's nagging away at me like something else on the list all day and all night because I know that I have to use it all up. Otherwise it will – shock horror! – go to waste. I look at the size of the oats order and realise at a

conservative estimate, even if I eat larger bowls of porridge than normal every day, that I will still be trying to use up this bag of porridge by February of next year, not even have one day off with a piece of toast or a boiled egg. Unless I do something mad which will increase the oat consumption like make some flapjacks or some granola bars. I like porridge naturally, but porridge every day between now and February is a little depressing. And the mango chunks. Yes, I like mango, but they're a bit, well, tinny, and the cranberry juice is good for you, granted, but frankly I don't like it. I serve up the first dish of Mexican bean soup, and everyone says they hate it. Don't even like beans. So now I have 12 tins of the soup and 24 of mung beans and no one in the house much likes beans. And it all cost over £50.

FIND FLAPJACK RECIPE

August 3rd

Mother-in-law visit imminent. To explain, the house gets dusted from top to bottom twice a year – once at Christmas and once in the summer when mother-in-law comes to stay. Christmas and birthday presents given by her have to be on show. Family heirlooms have to be checked, dusted and in some cases taken out of cupboards and put on display. Clothes are ironed, beds are made, floors are cleaned and polished. People are told not to swear, or watch Sky rubbish on TV, or use words like mingers or dodgy. She's on my case, as ever, making a few catty comments about working mothers and how much her darling son has to do around the house. It's hard not to answer back. But for once she has something cheery to say, something that speaks volumes to me. She says, 'You know, you never really get over them leaving home, but it will get easier, and the longer she's away from you the more she'll realise how much she loves YOU.' Feel guilty about making such a fuss about her coming for the extra night.

To DO

Leg wax
Check flight times
Make list of things needed for holiday

August 5th

It's raining again. I find rain more annoying the older I get. Rain is not only obviously very disappointing if you are going to the races, or having a barbecue or getting married, but it's also annoying if you are just going about your daily business. Holding an umbrella is irritating, and if you wear your cagoule you look like a total saddo. It makes your hair frizzy, and in the car the windscreen wipers need constant attention: either they're on too fast or they're on too slow. What is it with them? Maybe I need to chill out more.

To DO

Buy waterproofs for holiday
Find list of things needed for holiday
Put waterproofs on the list
Put screen wash in car

August 7th

Have been browsing the Sunday supplements for bad-back aids for a while. There is a whole range to choose from. Now I am middle-aged I have the statutory bad back. I have to choose the height of my chair carefully, I can't sit for too long and feel stiff when I stand up . . . So I ordered one of those ludicrous contraptions you dangle upside down on, apparently it works like traction, pulls your whole back out in a stretch and your back is good as new or refund guaranteed. In the photo is a man in a cardigan happily dangling backwards from the waist in the living room, cool as you like, and he's reading a book... Mine arrived in a flat pack (naturally) and determined to get on it as soon as possible I made GRUMPY OLD MAN put it up immediately he got home. YOUNGEST and her friend and GOM dug in for the floor show and Yours Truly lies back and dangles, feeling very adventurous indeed. Sudden blood rush to head and stupid dizzy turn followed within a couple of seconds. Sniggers and told-you-sos all round. Now I have to put the whole thing back in the packaging and feel sick. Think I might have brought on a small stroke. Will stick to Pilates in future.

August 9th

Start my first serious pile of things in the spare room to take on holiday. Put my slippers in. I am actually taking my slippers on holiday. Scary.

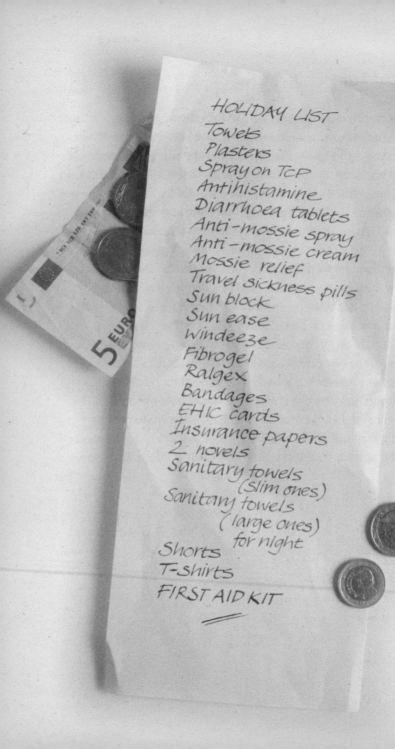

HOLIDAY LIST
Towels
Plasters
Spray on TCP
Antihistamine
Diarrhoea tablets
Anti-mossie spray
Anti-mossie cream
Mossie relief
Travel sickness pills
Sun block
Sun ease
Windeeze
Fibrogel
Ralgex
Bandages
EHIC cards
Insurance papers
2 novels
Sanitary towels
   (Slim ones)
Sanitary towels
   (large ones)
     for night
Shorts
T-shirts
FIRST AID KIT

August 10th

I'm getting really fed up with GOM's snoring. I mean I'm not sure what's happened here. Is it because I am now total saddo insomniac and I wake up and hear the appalling trumpeting sound and then can't get back to sleep, or does the trumpet solo wake me up in the first place, or is it just that he is annoying me more during daylight hours and therefore I now feel like poking him with that sharp meat fork by the oven that we use for picking up the Sunday roast. Which might be a marketing opportunity for a domestic tool of torture. A simple electric shock system whereby if he does start snoring then there's a short electric shock that wakes him up momentarily and trains his brain not to do it any more. Last night I was going to bed about ten minutes after him, except, guess what, he went straight up to bed after announcing he was going to bed – but I stopped to get some chops out of the freezer, filled the dog's water bowl, put cereal bowls out for breakfast, put some washing away and cleaned and flossed my teeth. My dreary tasks don't finish until my head hits the pillow, it seems, whereas his do . . . Got upstairs on to the landing and I could hear him from the top of the stairs, so I go in and say 'For God's sake you're snoring already' and he says, 'What . . . I'm not even asleep.' I'm sending him to the dentist to have one of those contraptions I saw a poster of in the waiting room to cure snoring; they wire up your jaws. Might ask for a key. Keep it. Like a modern-day chastity belt. Only release him when his mother comes round.

To DO
Find holiday list
Add:
Sandals
Sunhat
new sunglasses
Find holiday booking form –
    do we have twin beds ?

August 11th

The sun is shining. It is a gorgeous day. And YOUNGEST and her friend are watching satellite TV again. Another make-over show . . . hundreds of gay men and stupid women who look like Britney or Paris Hilton in silly short skirts and sounding the end of every sentence up like a question. Flicking their hair back and showing off. My mother used to complain about me watching TV when it was nice weather. I remember her doing that. I also remember not getting it. Truly not understanding it. At least I was only watching Rolf Harris and *Animal Magic*; these days children are watching extreme make-over and hideous American shows about blonde bimbos with liposuction.

To DO
Buy badminton rackets
Look at National Trust family
            days-out website.

August 12th

Keep thinking I can smell gas in the downstairs loo. Other people have mentioned it too. But this morning it was horrendous. So rang the number at the front of the telephone book for emergency gas leaks. Satisfyingly fast pick-up, urgent and diligent answer, if only everyone answered the phone like this. Especially to *me*. Described symptoms and they said they'd be round within the hour. Turn everything off! Go into emergency mode! Put the radio on! Huddle in pairs! Get all your stocks of baked beans out, blankets, everything. No, well, not that then . . . But that was the tone of it. I'm ashamed to say that it feels quite nice – if I was prone to hoaxing, which I'm not, I can see the attraction, the ultimate attention-seeking ploy, and they were here in 20 minutes, obviously expecting some major explosion.

They arrive in wonderfully important-looking van. Baffled engineers after about an hour lift a manhole cover by the downstairs loo. The foreman tells me we have sewer gas. I look puzzled. He has to explain in simple terms. Which is code for smelly and I imagine big poos down our drains. No more Suma orders for us!

To Do
Join National Trust
Air freshener
Bleach

August 14th

Leave house at 4.30am – why is it that every holiday I have
ever gone on involves a ghastly in-the-middle-of-the-night early
start? Living at the end of runway of Terminal 4 at Heathrow
airport would be only way of avoiding this it seems, since
airlines are so determined to get you to the airport hours before
strictly necessary. We are off on a very unusual holiday: with
ELDEST being away and YOUNGEST wanting adventure,
decided to book a canoeing holiday in the Dordogne. In the
brochure it looks wonderful. The Dordogne is obviously a very
wide calm river, and the canoes we will be driving are big
canoes that look more like punts than canoes; I know all this
because I studied the photos in the brochure very carefully
indeed before booking it.

We shall be able to meander down the river all morning, take
a lazy lunch, meander some more, then stroll to our nice hotel
for an overnight stay. Life jackets are optional, so they can't be
expecting rough whitewater, and YOUNGEST is a little bit
excited. Job done. Says all you need is an instruction hour on
Day One with group leader, then off you all go, small children
can take their own canoe out on their own, with Mum and Dad
following. In other words it's child's play, anyone can do it.

The rep meets us in the airport, carrying a sign saying
Canoeing Adventures. I feel very adventurous indeed. ELDEST is
off in Ghana and we are having our own adventure Enid Blyton
or *Swallows and Amazons* fashion. YOUNGEST will chum up
with other teenagers and I will feel sense of achievement and
enough fresh air to last me until next Easter. There is another
family gathering with the rep, but they're carrying all sorts of
equipment, as in waterproof holders, caskets, picnic bags, and

have brought their own safety helmets and oars. Panic number one; are we supposed to bring our own gear? No, the Bronningtons have done it before, they are master canoeists, will be doing our week to warm up then some whitewater stuff after. They seem nice enough, they're from Cardiff, luckily they have two teenage daughters so it is all seeming to fall into place nicely.

We get to the hotel and there are maps and an induction leaflet to read, and the inevitable risk assessment form, the one that says Canoeing Adventures are not liable if you canoe yourself into a rock and die, or are permanently disfigured by canoe or paralysed by both; the one that says in fact it's all your fault anyway. A flutter of nerves. Then I read the descriptions of each day's canoeing, with a key to what the levels of difficulty mean . . . Day 1 is easy canoeing, just some gentle rapids. Day 2 is gentle, some interesting rapids to 'keep you awake', and includes on the map some serious instructions not to take

ASK AT
RECEPTION
WHAT THE
EQUIVALENT
OF 999
IS HERE

certain branches of river because they do actually go to some really quite dangerous rapids. Already I am worrying about taking the wrong turn because I am quite capable of taking the wrong turn and almost certainly will. Day 3, it says, OK you've had two days of fun, now for the hard stuff, four hours' hard canoeing, partly upstream, with some really exciting rapids and whitewater; Day 5, now you are an expert it will seem like a doddle but this one takes in part of the Olympic training ground for canoeing; watch out for some really challenging rock avoidance work. You wanted an adventure holiday, well you got one!

Find it hard to sleep that night with worry.

August 15th

Day 1 of canoeing holiday. After an early breakfast the bus takes three groups – including the expert Bronningtons – to start of route, while our luggage is taken on to first hotel. On the way in the bus we go parallel to the river, and I ask if we are going to be canoeing on the bits we can see. The answer is yes. The road swings over on bridges here and there, everyone else looks at the river, and the canoeists already on it, with excitement. I look at it in horror, they are not paddling along like it looked in the photo in the brochure, as if they are in a paddling pool in Sutton Park or on a municipal boating lake, they are paddling hard, going round rocks, racing down speedy lanes that go round corners and suchlike. Crikey, this looks infinitely more difficult than I thought! Out we get and Charles our teacher shows us the canoes that are going to be ours for the next week. And the barrels we are to put all our daily valuables in, which are watertight containers. Helmets are handed round – hold on, I

thought this was just a jolly cruise. – life jackets are issued and
signed for. More legal documents to sign. Charles says they've
tightened the rules since the brochure went to print. I am afraid
to ask why. Still, at least Charles our teacher is coming with us, I
shall just have to be teacher's pet for the week, follow him,
watch the way he paddles his paddle and do the same, become
teacher's twin. Alas, Charles informs me he is just here to give us
an hour's lesson and then bog off to sort out the Cycling for
Softies lot who have just arrived too.

Cycling for Softies suddenly seems like an infinitely better
alternative and to think I discounted it on the basis that it might
be a bit too hot for cycling – what was I thinking of? A bit hot
feels like easy-peasy by comparison. The Bronningtons get out
all their annoying canoe gear, like they think they are in the
Olympic team, waterproof map containers, compasses,
lightweight holdalls and wetsuits with brilliantly clever
waterproof shoes. We look like the amateurs that we are: shorts,
sandals and sleeveless tops. Not that sunburn is top of my list of
worries at the moment. First Charles gives us a dry land lesson.
Dos and don'ts, how to get in and how to get out, how to make
sure you keep hold of your oars, and how to strap down your
waterproof barrel with your passport, camera and money in. OK
I might be all right, for goodness' sake there are four-year-olds
doing it. We get a canoe each off the rack, and it weighs a ton,
YOUNGEST and GOM have decided to share a canoe and I am
on my own, which is probably just as well
since I can see that I am going to be a bit of
a handful. Have to get Charles to help
me down with mine, and establish
myself as Miss Needy. He tells us to
all get in the water and start getting

used to it, and he'll help us with steering and run through the safety stuff. Everyone else is in the water in a jiffy, having fun, zipping in and out, and to my dismay the Bronningtons get in their canoes and whizz straight off . . . say they know the safety briefing off by heart, so there isn't even going to be anyone else to follow, and so much for YOUNGEST palling up with their kids . . . I will have to follow GOM and YOUNGEST and they will soon get fed up with me. Charles takes us through how to steer right and left, for some reason it seems like the opposite way to the way I would logically expect to do it, and the more I think about it the worse I get. GOM and YOUNGEST are larking about in their boat, doing twirls one-handed, and I am getting myself into a top-of-the-range flap.

Charles takes me off for some individual tuition, which is what I had hoped, tells me I'll be fine, the water is only about 6 foot deep max, been doing the holidays for years, never been a mishap. Enjoy it.

Off he goes, the others go on ahead and I say not to leave me behind . . . But they do anyway. I start to get the hang of it, the scenery is fantastic, and the trees go by, the water is fab. We all stop and we have a swim, this is a true adventure – gosh, I feel wonderful, it's exactly what we needed to do, the three of us together. Get back in feeling on top of the world, we are halfway to the next stopping point and a third of the way to the hotel stop. I can hear a bit of rushing water, the others glance back and look excited, I suddenly realise there isn't a brake, as in there is no way of stopping.

I can feel the water pulling me towards the rushing water, feel it making me go a bit faster. There are no trees to hang on to, so I start practising which way to do the oar to make me turn the corner or steer me round to the right bit of the river to go in the easy stream. The others go on the left-hand one, and they point at it for me to see, like, hey, you take the left one and turn round and carry on, the right-hand one doesn't look like it leads to Niagara Falls or anything but it does have some rocks sticking out. Suddenly rocks sticking out feel a bit scary since the water is pulling me faster and faster now. No choice, it will be fun, other people in the river ahead have obviously done it and survived – carried on chatting in fact, so off I go. Bit of adrenalin, a bit scared and you might know I put the oar in the wrong way, go down the right-hand side and one minute I am in boat, next I am under water, with all my belongings rushing down the river, nothing hurt, nothing seriously to worry about, but I am suddenly aware of how dangerous this whole thing is, narrowly miss. I catch one oar somehow, get to the side and hope that someone will pick up boat, oar and the rest of my belongings downstream. Get to the side and am very frightened. Other people glide past, some of them eating ice creams and one reading a magazine making it look very easy. I am not finding it easy.

It's very humiliating walking along a French dual carriageway sopping wet in your bathing costume carrying one oar. People stop and ask if you're OK, but this was the only choice. Charles said he was fine about finding canoe downstream and bringing it to the hotel. That's what he said but I could tell he thinks I am high-maintenance guest from hell.

To Do
Ask Charles if I can rope myself on
            to another canoe?

August 16th

Everyone tells me it's easy, I will get the hang of it, but since I capsized I have lost whatever nerve I had. But still there are six more canoeing days to go, so I have to get back in. First couple of hours of canoeing goes well, nice wide bits of the river, some beautiful scenery and lots of stretches where I practise which way to put the oar in to go right and left. I'll be fine. Then a stretch of fast water comes towards me, and this time there is an overhanging tree on the bend, I miss it by about half an inch, and this is a bit of a setback. There's no time to think, then straight into another couple of bends and I put the oar in the wrong side again but this time overcompensate for the mistake and end up – joy of joys – going round next bend backwards. I don't capsize, I bang into the side really badly, and get stuck with my boat sticking out and suddenly about 30 teenagers in canoes come at me and have to steer round my boat, causing mayhem and shouts and more scary near misses. That's it. I drag the boat out and wait for help. Which takes about three hours, when they finally notice I am missing at lunch stop.

Hand canoe in to Charles who looks relieved and I effectively become coat holder and person who spends the day at the hotel. Perhaps not such a bad outcome. My adventure holiday days are over.

August 17th

Lolled by pool all day worrying about GOM and YOUNGEST canoeing some tricky bits. They came back beaming – had a lovely day. Why do I find physical things so difficult when others clearly do not?

August 20th

Last day of holiday. OK I didn't manage the canoe but we had a lovely time the three of us. Dreaded hearing emergency bad news from Ghana, checking mobile whole time, but the dynamics of the family have changed with ELDEST not there. It makes me enjoy our family time together more than ever. Only 14 days till ELDEST comes home. Might make a banner.

To DO
Buy present for Mother-in-law, Mother
            and ELDEST from France
Find launderette for sopping wet clothes
Buy more Ralgex for GOM

September

September 1st

ELDEST is due home tomorrow. I would like to say that the seven weeks has whizzed by, but it emphatically has not – it has dragged. The process of giving her up to the world, which is effectively what this has been, has been hard, slow and reluctant on my part – it feels like she has been prised out of my hands for ever more. But judging by the (infrequent) emails, she has had the time of her life, had a truly amazing time, and of course who would deny their beloved child an experience like that? But now I am dying to see her, dreading a little seeing the mossie bites and the sunburn and the weight loss, all of which are inevitable, and for the last week I have thrown myself into Welcome Home mode – decide to throw a party, blow up balloons and paint banner for front door. Am truly excited. More excited than I can remember feeling for years. Like it's my fifth birthday party and I am expecting my first bike. I do something I can't remember doing since I was at university: I put some disco music on really really loud – Tina Turner's 'Nutbush City Limits' to be precise –

dance my heart away upstairs, really go for it, work up a sweat. YOUNGEST arrives home unheard and puts her head round the door; she tells me never to do that again. But I think I will.

TO DO
Make home-made pesto sauce for supper
   when ELDEST back and stock up on
                    HOB NOBS
Put flowers in her room
Buy cereal assortment pack

September 2nd

We drive to Heathrow and it feels like a whole year, never mind seven weeks, has passed since we took her there to see her off to Ghana. We park the car, my stomach feels churned up with excitement, I feel like shouting out at the top of my voice that my daughter is coming home. At the arrivals hall in Terminal 4 there is the usual crowd gathered – some drivers with signs for their clients, and some young parents with a baby holding a sign saying 'welcome home, Grandma!' presumably for someone who's just become a

grandmother. I start crying and I don't even know them. There are dozens of people just like us, looking for loved ones coming off planes from all over the world.

And out she comes with her trolley, looking a bit overwhelmed with all the crowd staring, but knowing that we are looking at her and seeing a grown-up woman, not a girl, knowing that that's what we're thinking, which we are. She is indeed blotchy with mossie bites, brown, bedraggled and a lot skinnier, but beaming – and to think that I wished her home so often – she is happy happy happy, and naturally I burst into tears. We get in the car and I can't help but overwhelm her with questions: 'OK so you got off the plane, then what?' type questions. She'll tell us in her own time.

At last I can stop reading the dreadful Foreign News pages of the *Guardian* and can luxuriate in the trusty *Daily Mail*. Can't stop smiling.

TO DO
Buy more washing powder
Call doctor about malaria symptoms

September 3rd

Saw something really extraordinary this morning by the bird table. A spotty bird with a long beak was picking up a snail shell and breaking it on the patio – slapping it down on to the stonework like a woman beating washing – then eating the snail inside. I had assumed that all the broken snail shells on the floor were result of GOM clumsily stepping with big trainers on snails when putting out bread for birds. But no, amazingly the bird –

whatever it is – is clever enough to pick them up and shake the snails out. Like someone using those fancy metal pliers in posh restaurant eating escargots. Surely this is evidence that birds are truly intelligent. Think I might put GOM's binoculars in kitchen for serious bird-spotting.

To Do
Buy more birdseed
Scrape bird poo off patio by bird table

September 4th

The beginning of term looms, and suddenly there is a stack of things to do to prepare for YOUNGEST's new school year. It's more of a backlog than a new stack to be precise, because I should have been busy with this pile of tasks way back in July. I know that because although it is early September the shops have been emptied of school shoes, green opaque tights, white ankle socks, rulers and protractor sets. Because organised mothers do these tasks immediately after the summer term finishes, whereas the rest of us are so worn out after a whole school year, we stuff it all in the spare room and bask in the joy of not having to get two kids to school, the kitchen tidied, three beds made and a dog walked before 7.40 and then resume school duties in early September.

Stay-at-home mothers, or worse the kind of mothers who have given up their high-powered job in the City to look after their children and are endlessly featured in the *Daily Mail*-type mothers, have got to the shops well before me. They did all these dreary tasks the moment the school broke up, probably badgered the school secretary for the autumn kit list even before it was sent out to parents. Because stay-at-home mothers are perfect. But the ones that have given up a high-powered job are easily the worst. Like ex-smokers, they can't stop talking about their brilliantly clever decision to put their family first, to live life to the full and play Junior Scrabble all afternoon – better still they opt to educate their children at home. Can't they just shut up about it all? I imagine they do feel they did the right thing, well OK, but most of us don't frankly have the choice. We've got mortgages, we've got careers that it took us a lifetime to achieve and frankly we don't want to spend all day buffing up the toaster or sorting out the family photos and teaching our children algebra (or whatever they do in maths today). We like to get out of the house, and put some nice clothes on and a pair of heels and have a coffee with someone at work we like – we want to do all this as well as be great mothers. So what's wrong with that? Sadly, having both still seems as elusive as ever and at this time of year the madness of it all is at its most apparent.

Buying a pair of school shoes is a bad task at the best of times, but factor in a teenage daughter and it's one of the lowest points of the calendar year. I pick out the black sensible ones – I don't mean the clompy lace-ups or the Start Rite ones, I'm not that stupid – but obviously the days when I could basically impose my own choice of shoes on my daughters are long gone . . . Now it's a battle of wills. Who is able to stand off for longest. YOUNGEST is determined to have a pair with heels that will make her swagger along and the boys watch her cute little bum. Because we are entering the snogging-on-the-corner-by-the-newsagents-before-you-go-into-school sort of era. There are no doors to slam at the shoe shop, but if there were then YOUNGEST would slam at least a couple during the process. Of course she holds the trump card, which is that she says she doesn't care if she goes back to school in the old sloppy, scuffed, ruined ones from last term, nor does she care how long it takes to trudge round all the shops – she has all the time in the world, relatively. My patience with shops is very short indeed, my attention span even shorter. So she knows that sooner or later I will give in, it will just be a matter of who cracks first. We come out of the fourth shop unable to agree on anything like a compromise. Needless to say, by shop six it's me that cracks. We buy a pair of shoes with heels that in my view are far too high.

Came home and spent half an hour in the kitchen putting all the glasses in size order – wineglasses, tumblers, small tumblers – all in fabulous neat rows facing front of cupboard. Annoyed that some rows had odd numbers, but all in all it made me feel better. Kept opening the cupboard door to admire my work. Pathetic. Felt my life in better more organised shape as a result.

To DO
Buy 3 more wine (goblet shape) glasses
1 small tumbler
Order school skirt
Find name tags
Find school reading list – hunt in
      dressing-table drawers

September 6th

YOUNGEST goes back to school. Stupidly I agreed to her taking in packed lunches this term, on the condition that she has to do them all herself – plan them and prepare them the night before. The first day it's all neatly wrapped in silver foil, in Tupperware and by the front door as agreed the night before. I wonder how long it will last? Stay-at-home mothers again don't allow such things, no matter how much their children plead, their children remain on school dinners. Only working mothers with guilt give in to such nonsense and make a rod for their own backs. YOUNGEST goes back to school in trophy new high-heeled shoes and guess what, comes home, kicks them off and announces everyone is into flatties, why didn't I make her buy a pair of them? And they hurt and can she have some more plasters to take to school with her?

Jocasta sends me an email reminding me that my performance review is later this month. Will make sure I am at work 15 minutes earlier for next couple of weeks, might send her an email on Sunday night, show off that I often work at home at weekends. Which I don't.

TO DO
Finish off report on management
                                    restructure
Set alarm 15 minutes earlier

September 7th

The programme for evening classes comes through the door like it always does at this time of year. With the usual offerings . . . Bookkeeping for Beginners, Accountancy and Computer Skills for the Afraid, and a new one, eBay for Beginners. So that's how people get the hang of it. They take a course in it. Wouldn't just going shopping be a whole lot easier? However, one class does catch my eye since I have a big belly and I like dancing, so I sign up to Belly Dancing sample night.

TO DO
Find hobby
Sandwich fillers for packed lunch
Binoculars

September 9th

Packed lunch regime already slipping. She left it till last minute this morning and I had to do it. There's a surprise.

Belly dancing night. I seem to be the only one trying it out, and everyone else is a regular. The regulars including 'Miss' are warming up, doing amazing stretches and bendy things on mats to music that sounds like you should be ordering a lamb pasanda. Makes me want a lamb pasanda, which is not really the idea. Miss gives me a mat and I try to join in their bendy bits and fail. She claps her hands and the group get changed. They put on some floaty skirts with jangly bits around the hip and one lady pulls out a full costume, a marvellous swirly purple job and a veil or two. They are all big women, and I feel I might have hit on something really good for me – something expressive and fun and a bit sexy for the woman who is a size 16 and over. Something akin to dancing upstairs to Tina Turner when you think no one is looking, but doing it legitimately. Miss says it's free expression tonight. She puts on a piece of music and says we all have to concentrate on a life force travelling up from our middle to third toe, up the back of our ankle, through our groin and up to our left nipple. 'Let yourselves go.' Far from learning how to shake my booty big time, or the equivalent of pole dancing for the plump, it's all very moody, everyone goes into their own individual trance, some of them with their veils on, circling and skipping round the assembly hall a bit like a lot of grown-ups doing music and movement but not in their vests like we did when I was little. Miss says to relax and enjoy it. Most of them have their eyes closed, and I pretend to close mine but have a sneaky look at them and try to look like I am fully relaxed and expressing myself to the music. Some of them are really going for it, especially I imagine when their energy line gets to the groin. Which seems to be happening for everyone except me.

After about five minutes of doing the whirling dervishes Miss claps her hands and then asks everyone pretty much how it was for them. Did they feel the energy? What sort of feelings came up? Did they feel mischievous, or closed or youthful? They compare notes and experiences and I pretend to look at the floor and fiddle in my bag. She reads out what they were supposed to feel. Talks about the yin and yang and the elements involved – fire, water and so on – and off they go again with music number two. This goes on for a good hour and a half.

Miss asks me if I want to sign up for a course of ten and I make my excuses and leave. Alas, it felt as though they were all having a group orgy and I was trying to get myself into the zone but failing miserably, a bit like trying to have an orgasm when you realise you've left the immersion on or a baked potato in the oven. Far from making me more relaxed I came home more tense than ever.

To DO
Ask school about tickets to YOUNGEST's
                    musical
find chimney sweep's number
firelighters

September 12th

GET HOBBY

I persuade ELDEST to come on a pamper day with me – a girly treat before she goes away to university next week. I wouldn't exactly say she was enthusiastic but interestingly, she would never have agreed to it so readily before the Ghana experience – she'd have pulled a face and said 'not really' and I would have lost my nerve and not pushed it – but this time she said OK in a way that meant, yes – really OK – and we go along to the local golf club hotel and get kitted out in the white towelling dressing gowns and the silly free slippers that trip you up as you walk. Maybe we'll turn into those mothers and daughters who shop together on a Saturday and link arms. That might be taking things too far.

The idea of a pamper day is obviously to relax, but I have lost the ability to relax. Even when I go out of my way to try and relax, it doesn't happen – in fact, especially if I go out of my way to relax it doesn't happen. For a start, the other women on the pamper day are annoying. They got there ten minutes before us, probably know the drill inside out and have bagsied all the sunloungers – which gets me all wound up straight away – and they keep their towels and their silly magazines on them even while they're having lunch. Which I think should be disallowed or illegal. I mean, why should you keep a sunlounger for the day, in your possession? Either you are using it to lie on or you're not. I sit and seethe about it, consider suggesting to the management that each sunbed should have a little disc on it, like disabled parking badges, so that you put the time on that you vacate your sunbed to go to the loo, or to the sauna, or to have your nails painted, and if the time vacated exceeds 30 minutes then your possessions should be folded neatly on the floor and the sunbed vacated for other pampees. Marvellous system. The very model of democracy. I don't say anything, don't make a fuss or a scene, about it, and unusually let it lie. I am trying to impress ELDEST daughter after all.

The women doing the pampering are like hairdressers only worse, they will insist on trying to talk to you all the time. I don't want to talk to them. At all. With their candles and silly whale music and the twigs that have been curled in reception.

She covers me from head to toe in oil – I'm like a basted turkey and feel about as attractive. The daft music comes on that's supposed to get you in the relaxation zone, but just gets you more wound up and irritable. Then she does something ridiculously pretentious like put a warm pebble on my forehead and it's all I can do not to laugh but that would offend her. So I pretend it's done the trick and pretend to be very very relaxed indeed.

Which is hard since she's seeing bits of me normally hidden from the outside world. With good reason. Instead of relaxing, I worry for her. Poor girl's prodding and poking my nooks and crannies. You'd have to be cut out for it.

Despite all the grump going on in my head about the pamper

day experience, ELDEST and I had a lovely time. I was very careful not to ask too many questions about her personal life, like it said in the *Daily Mail* article about empty nesters, and little bits of information started to trickle out as the article said they would . . . That she would miss her little sister – a bit – when she went away to university, and that next summer she wants to go to Africa to do what effectively sounds like modern missionary work. Am simultaneously proud and dismayed. The eight-week gap experience was merely the beginning. I have to make my life my own from now on. It's not going to be easy.

To Do

Book holiday for GOM and me
Find out about politically dangerous
                              regions in Africa

September 13th

  Jocasta calls me in for the dreaded Annual Performance
Review. Dreaded not because I think she will sack me or demote
me, but just because the whole thing is such a farce. She hands
over the set of objectives, targets and achievements that we
jointly agreed on last year. I find myself glaring at her
coathanger on the back of her office door. Might sneak in one of
my size 18 ones to replace her size 14 when she is out and that
way Robin will see it and think she is really a size 18. Neat idea I
think. I do my prepared speech about what I feel I have
achieved and she looks a bit bored – swear I saw one of her
nostrils start to flare – and she winds it up in about 15 minutes.
No idea what contribution she makes at all, no idea what the
point of it was, except to tick some boxes . . . See now I'm
starting to talk like everyone else in the silly Office Language . . .
At the end of it I ask if she could consider please a pay rise, not
unreasonably, but she looks a bit taken aback – hello? – and says
she can see no justification for it whatsoever, unless – and it
looked like she was clutching at straws – I feel like becoming the
Departmental Fast Response Officer, which is office speak for
first aid person, which Head Office now insist on. I find myself
agreeing to it. Me, first aid, I can't even watch *Animal Hospital*
with both eyes open.

To Do
Look out medical book
Find out what pay supplement
          will be if I do course
Order new kitchen catalogue

September 16th

There's a quality of light about autumn, a slight change in the angle of the sun which casts a familiar light over the place – the condensation starts, little messages go on the kitchen calendar that say dreary things like get boiler serviced, or clean gutters above kitchen, service lawnmower and other such delights, things that mean inevitably the long long winter is on its way. You have your first fire. Eat your first crumpet. Write your first Christmas list. Because I am so old and because I have been there, done that, got the T-shirt, it feels like only five minutes ago I was doing the same things last year. The seasons come round so fast, and I recognise the smell of bonfires, the colours of the leaves, the early-morning mists, and know that this means autumn. Time goes so slowly when you're young, drags and moves like treacle, and now time simply runs so fast like lightning. Where did all the time go, and how did I get to be this middle-aged? Suddenly there isn't that much of my life left, and I can't shake off the feeling that I am still trying to get things right, get the balance of things right, get the hang of making proper gravy and being able to hold a decent conversation about the Pre-Raphaelites.

Go for glorious walk on the coast and bump into some lovely ramblers who are listening to a curlew. They show me the curlew and point out its amazing song. Now I can show off about curlews to my heart's content. Better – even – than showing off about the Pre-Raphaelites!

curlew

To Do
Buy new walking boots
Look up curlew in bird book
Join National Trust
Organise long walk for Sunday week

September 17th

We drive ELDEST up to Aberdeen, the car packed full of her clothes, jewellery, shoes, mugs and little knick-knacks she is taking to personalise her room. GOM manages the drive all the way up there without any nagging or interrogation at all, talks about politics, Africa, pop music, and it is left to me to ask her about registering with the student doctor, checking her insurance and to remember to buy fruit regularly. I know it doesn't do me any good, but I can't stop myself.

Once we get to the Hall of Residence it becomes very hard indeed. Seems like the day before yesterday that I was going through the exact same thing with my own parents. We get to the second floor and the moment she sees another student she wants us gone, urgently. We bring the stuff up, the two of us in shifts, and know that we need to be gone as fast as possible. Your parents are a liability in this context. We scarper fast. But as soon as we are out of sight GOM pulls over in a lay-by and we both cry our eyes out.

Get home to find my mother has left some flowers and a note for me saying, 'She'll be back, and when she does come back she'll appreciate you all the more. Love Mum.'

To DO
Take my mother out more.
Pick up my mother's prescription

September 23rd

The HRT pills don't seem to be making any difference to my mood, but if anything I am more weepy. Prone to sobbing at the most ridiculous things like soppy adverts, or soppy birthday cards, or to my astonishment Rolf Harris singing 'Two Little Boys'. Go back to doctor and say I might need to stop the HRT since it's not working – I go from high as a kite to down in the dumps in about three seconds flat, can cry at the drop of a hat, and it is still making my libido go berserk. Assumed she would get me back on the menstrual mood diary-keeping again, but she simply tells me to go home and take up a hobby. I suppose some of my menstrual mood diaries were a bit over the top. Came home and made some plum jam, put it all in neat, clean little jam jars and then whizzed into town to buy some of those cute home-made jam labels   I put two of the best jars on one side to take up to Dundee for the first time we go to see ELDEST. It's spookily just what my mother did. Hormones have a way of overriding even HRT it seems. Perhaps I am turning into a nice old lady.

To DO
Write 'Gratitude List' like it said in
          GOOD HOUSEKEEPING

September 25th

The farmers' market comes to town. I see some like-minded women running a stall called the Farmers' Wives. They have those nice ruched white collar blouses and Barbours on, and they've made some wonderful home-made lemon and apple tarts and home-made Bakewells. I envy them. They probably all have a large kitchen with a big Aga and some lambs warming, and a strapping farmer for a husband who comes in from the cold at 4pm and flops in front of the telly. A bloke who knows how to bleed a radiator, is good with his hands and has a ruddy complexion. Life would be simple, if a little predictable, the Farmers' Wives meetings would be cheery, the profit going to their annual cheese and wine evening, or a ploughman's lunch quiz night. But being a farmer's wife you could man the teas and coffees, be busy putting up the ploughman's lunches at the hatch while everyone else was trying to answer the difficult questions. I recognise the fact that this little fantasy of mine is not real, but I imagine that their lives are relatively simple compared to mine. That they don't have to bother with too many emails or reports or deadlines, or office politics or anything of that nature. And that they live on the edge of some gorgeous wood or coppice and their children come home for Sunday lunch with their families. You'd think at my age I would have stopped thinking that the grass is always greener, stopped thinking that other people's lives are more perfect, more happy

than my own. Alas, with age it hasn't got much better. The only thing I have learned is that the simpler your life the happier you are. The simpler your targets, the happier with a capital H you are. And their Bakewells are to die for.

TO DO
Write 'Gratitude List'
Evening Primrose Oil

October

October 1st

Activity on the bird table is becoming rather sparse, only a couple of robins and a black thing with an orange beak today. I suppose with it being a bit colder they are hiding in their nests and stocking up for winter – or is that squirrels? I point this out as a matter of educational interest to YOUNGEST, saying how fascinating that they are probably spending more and more time in their nests, are about to hibernate, and she tells me with a mouth full of cereal, 'They've migrated, dur' (yet another biology lesson I did not pay enough attention to at school it seems), so I tidy the binoculars away upstairs.

Once you have a pair of binoculars in your hands it's hard not to use them. On anything at all. Inevitably I find myself looking over next door's fence, pointlessly scrutinising their hosepipes and lawnmower, and then pan over the back hedge and into the garden of the people whose house we back on to. They have a shed, so I try to see what they keep in it. I'm not even really that interested but the fact that I might be able to see in makes me want to see in.

Apparently blokes use their sheds for soft porn, so look for
evidence of such. Then scan over and I can see someone digging in
garden two doors away – I watch undetected . . . experience
shameful thrill, have to get a grip and realise that this newfound
interest in binoculars could get me in serious trouble. Maybe this
explains why middle-aged people get into birdwatching in the
first place, a harmless excuse to wander around with a pair of
binoculars round your neck. It almost certainly explains the
popularity of the Neighbourhood Watch scheme. Nothing to do
with dreary meetings about dog fouling and everything to do with
having an excuse to sit at the spare-room window with a pair of
binoculars poking your nose into other people's lives.

TO DO

Read up on bird migration
Look into more powerful binoculars

October 2nd

The first day of my two-day induction course as First
Response Officer. We have all been sent to Leeds – I assume that

since I am the most anxious catastrophiser person I know that I shall be top of class, maybe get home early since so much of the looking out for danger in everyday situations will be second nature for me, since this is what I do already. But alas, we are handed a huge introductory pack to familiarise ourselves with for tomorrow morning. Already I am beginning to think that the pitiful annual increment on offer will hardly be worth the hassle. Judging by the weight of the pack which we are told to read for tomorrow, which covers everything from do-it-yourself tracheotomies to basic midwifery, this course is not really meant to teach you anything but to tick boxes. OK it stops short of do-it-yourself amputation, which is thankfully unlikely in an open-plan HR office. Fair dos I suppose someone might conceivably fall out of the window down all six floors . . . but one would hope that someone would have the sense to dial 999 instead of calling the resident First Response Officer.

Apart from anything else, I might be good at worrying about potential dangers in everyday situations, but am pitifully squeamish, so I would almost certainly have passed out either with the sight of the blood or the sheer scale of the seriousness of the situation. I'm having trouble even looking at the diagrams in this manual. No one could be expected to read this tome overnight. No – this is about companies covering themselves for blame. They send someone on a residential course, give them a badge and a pay increase, and then if someone did trip over someone else's filing or electrocute themselves on the hand dryer in the ladies, the employer would be able to reduce their liability. Trouble is, I could do with the pay increase like everyone else, so here we are, all 15 of us, gathered at the bar, away from our families in a dreary out-of-town motel. I stay as long as is necessary and leave, having had considerable trouble balancing on the bar stool – I shall soon be so old people will bring me a chair to sit on at social gatherings and then abandon me. Which if I'm honest sounds quite good, then I wouldn't have to make so much small talk. I guess the next step on the I-am-too-old-to-be-sociable scale is pretending you are a bit deaf. Neat idea.

I loll in bed watching *Newsnight* – I say watching but now that ELDEST is back in the UK and I'm not on third world disaster alert, I don't really concentrate on any of the proper news. I'm really just looking at Jeremy Paxman and wondering whether his cute ties are ones he chooses himself or does his wife or partner do that for him, and if so what does that say about him and their relationship? Have never noticed him with wifey in the gossip columns. Even if she's indifferently pretty she'll have a Double First from Oxford – Paxman's not stupid. Fall asleep not having got any further than the section on Strain Injury and wake up at 02.16 to find the telly's still on and hideously hot room. Wish I was at home and that I hadn't agreed to do this silly course. And also wish I hadn't eaten Pringles from minibar.

To Do
Prepare an intelligent question
                     about strain injuries
Buy GOM new tie

October 3rd

The woman who is running the stupid course is a little gender unspecific. She's wearing ghastly gabardine trousers and has a belt with a leather attachment for a mobile, a toggle would not look out of place or a whistle, and she's a bit scary. Hope there's not too much practical role play work. The first thing she does is she gets us to close our information pack and look at her, then she holds up a felt tip marker pen, and she asks us all to tell her what it is – no one says anything. Let's start again. I repeat . . . What is this?' It's like being at the panto but without the choc ice. 'A pen. Thank you, yes, a pen, at last.' Then she throws the marker pen on the floor. And then she says, 'OK, now tell me what it is.' We look even more perplexed than when she held it up in the first place. One of us sheepishly says, 'A pen on the floor.' 'Come on, you lot, wakey wakey. What is it now?' No one has the faintest idea what she is getting at. 'A hazard. Repeat after me, a hazard . . . A pen on the floor is a hazard. Why? Because someone can slip on it, someone could have a fall, and who's fault would it be, whose responsibility is it to look out for such things? Yours!'

On and on she goes, bossing us about and flipping over charts and doing Powerpoint presentations about hazards and potential hazards, and then she shows us a risk assessment video. We all look like we might have a bit of a snooze in the dark, but apparently an exam follows . . . We have to watch it and assess the potential risks; we have to imagine we are setting up a circus tent in Harrogate, and it is the most complicated scenario imaginable involving crowd control, toxic gases, seat scaffolding and wild animals. Which all seems absurdly irrelevant since the riskiest office procedure we are likely to be assessing is changing the photocopier ink cartridge or finding an extension lead. The inevitable multiple choice questionnaire follows. Why is it with multiple choices there is never a box that says 'it depends' or 'maybe' or 'sometimes'? My score is pitifully low, not because I have ignored potential hazards but because I have rated everything as high risk. I'm anxious about everything. A modern-day Captain Mainwaring, hopeless in a

tips to beat tiredness

energy ebbing

Vitamins & Minerals

Vitamins and minerals in the right...
...and combinations are vital to good...
And the best way to obtain them is...
...food you eat, although there are...
...ment and mineral supplements...
...are to talk to your doctor if...

Vitamins & Minerals

Vitamins and minerals sometimes need to be eaten in combinations to make a difference. eg

Vitamin C helps **iron** to be more easily absorbed, so a glass of orange juice first thing in the morning...
...is a Vit C) with a boiled egg (for iron) again...
...is a good combination. A healthy...

Vitamin B6 is necessary to work properly...
Try natural butter, which contains all those...

Vitamin B6, **zinc** and **magnesium**...
Cereal, nuts...
Brazil nuts...
...which work together with...
...against disease...
...for healthy bones)...

folic acid (for healthy...

Vitamin B6...
...magnesium) helps the body absorb...
...calcium (found in fish bones and bread)...

Vitamin D (found in sardines and...
...which helps provide calcium...

calcium...

...foods like cereals) a better...

...with **fat**...

...dressing makes...

Breast Cancer Care
Marie Curie Cancer Care

essential guide
breast awareness

At Slimming World we don't advocate
that thin is beautiful. We want to help you
reach the weight that's right
not just now, but for life.

personal
achievement
target

...any to t...
...ut try bringin...
Sit with your eye...
your way round yo...
...The trick is to f...
...three as yo...

...tell

When you achieve your PAT you w...
a certificate. You are then entitled
class free as long as you stay within
...ow your PAT weight or until

...more below yo...

Health
your D...
...comp...
...be...

crisis, too panicked and nervous to be any use to anyone at all.

The afternoon First Aid sessions ends with a home-made splint and I think I am going to keel over; my imagination has simply run into overdrive. Severed bones, arteries and limbs fill my frenzied mind and I have to go and lie down in their First Aid room for half an hour to compose myself. Bossy Boots rings head office and I am sent home. Wasn't much of a pay increase anyway.

To DO
Cancel Boden order
Cancel appointment with kitchen designer
Save money

October 4th

ELDEST is coming home from university for the first time for the weekend. I clear the diary – take a couple of days off on Friday and Monday, get the fridge stocked up, make her favourite home-made chocolate mousse, and plan some nice walks for the three of us while YOUNGEST is at school. We could go blackberrying. She comes home Friday lunchtime, we tell her with some enthusiasm that we've booked a table at her favourite Chinese, and she says sorry she's arranged to see Lucy and Phoebe. She won't be needing any food till Sunday.

Feel foolish. She has come home principally to see her mates – yes, OK, I dare say it's nice for her to be home, but she's hardly been pining for us the way we have for her, and so it should be of course. But it's a hard lesson to learn.

This year I need to make Christmas the best ever. Christmas is a time when even birds who have flown the nest return.

To Do
organise family weekend away
Make Christmas cake

October 5th

I decide to go to a food allergist. Since I spend the whole time
with a stomach the size of a beach ball. It can't be (just) that I
am eating too much. OK it could be that. But every magazine I
open involves people finding out that they have food
intolerances. Celebrity after celebrity talking about their wheat
and dairy intolerance, and how their lives have changed as a
result. It's not cheap, as in an astonishing £50 for an hour
session, but the promise of reducing bloated stomach means
that money is no object. Even in the North, where I live, she is
booked up for every Saturday in the foreseeable future, so I am
not the first to catch on to the trend. She's at the back of the
hippy shop, the one with all the jangly chime bells and the kind
of clothes hippies wore in the early seventies, baggy ones, which
is an attractive quality, but if I wore them I would look like Gipsy
Rose Lee.

I assumed I would be painted with teeny neat samples of
tomato, cheese and yeast up my arm, but find instead it is a long
long list of questions about what I eat and how often, and she
wants detailed explanation of bowel movements. It's not as bad
as the woman on telly who pokes around in people's poo to
establish their diet regime, but it's not far off. Then she cuts a
great dollop of my hair off and sends it for analysis. Which
makes me a bit suspicious. Surely that's a lot of old nonsense,
isn't it? Being able to tell so much from a lob of hair? Suppose it
might be state-of-the-art DNA test but see no sign of white lab

coats. Wish I wasn't so cynical. She then goes on and on and on about how flour has changed over the centuries and claims that most of the Western world is now officially allergic to flour. Something to do with shelf life and additives. It makes sense. But surely we'd all be writhing in agony if we were all allergic to it. She is 99 per cent sure that what I have is a wheat allergy and so I am to give up pasta, bread, flour of any sort, except for the wheat-free stuff. She says everyone loses weight. Count me in.

TO DO
Find rye flour
Non-wheat pasta

GET
"RAT RACE"

October 7th

YOUNGEST's birthday is less than a month away and I haven't even started buying her presents. I know she wants a DVD called *The Rat Race*, so send GOM out to buy it. Tell him he must get it by the end of the week, consider it officially passed over, ticked off, done, delegated. I make him write it down. Sigh of relief, feel suddenly in front, ahead of the game. Marvellous.

October 8th

Got a bit maudlin. Sat on a wall overlooking forest at the end of our lane, and got a bit pensive. Realised how the year has flown by. I had been here in this exact spot, at this exact time of day, walking the dog back in the spring, which felt like five minutes ago, and so much has happened since . . . It's now late autumn, and with a flash of wisdom and panic combined I realise that I am now in the late autumn of my life as well – got to be two-thirds of the way through. I am shocked and horrified and return home with sense of urgency to enjoy life more.

Life is now officially in short supply. I resolve to change my approach to it as a result which obviously won't last . . . Must relax, must chill out, must learn Italian, must get more out of life, must see the Victoria Falls, must be happy, must do something significant today and then again tomorrow too. Life is running out, and there's loads of things I still want to do. Might do something mad like go off with Derek from Derek's shoe bar, or set myself up in a B and B on the Scilly Isles or turn into mad ageing hippy and sell home-made jam on trestle table at the end of the garden.

October 9th

You don't think it's going to happen to you. You were part of the generation who invented sex, you had a pair of hot pants, some Mary Quant shiny patent boots, you invented free love, you were around at the start of the Beatles. Surely you would be exempt? Catalogue addiction wouldn't happen to you. Then one day when your guard is down, when your concentration lapses, you phone up an ad in the *Sunday Times* for a rambling holiday brochure in the Tyrol, or you buy a useful shopping bag that folds up and zips inside your handbag, or some pants from M & S that are as big as a parachute, or you walk out of a shop with the most hideous cardigan on earth, probably in beige, and then it's too late. Someone in marketing catches on, gets your postcode and notices you are middle-aged . . . There is no going back.

The catalogues start coming. They know where you live, they know you have hit middle age, and they know what you want. Now. Probably make you want them. Inside you are still a sex kitten, still a groovy chick who can strut your stuff on the dance floor to Tina Turner . . . but to everyone else you are now just a middle-aged old cow with bad hair and bad jumpers. And the marketing geniuses who design catalogues seek you out like a heat-seeking missile, because they know that it may not be tomorrow or the day after, but some day relatively soon you are going to want to send off for a car boot tidy or a machine-washable beige dressing gown or a microwaveable hot-water bottle. And like all marketing geniuses, they're right. Something catches your eye, a jaunty but practical summer skirt, an attractive but serviceable gingham tablecloth that looks fresh and clean – it's no good fighting it, you can't win.

But the one made for grumpy old women, the one that hits the equivalent of our G spot, the one that is the weapon of mass destruction, the one that is guaranteed to wear you down and get you hooked is the Lakeland catalogue. Full of the kind of gadgets and handy items that appeal to the woman with too much to do, and whose house is a disorganised mess, and who would like it to be organised domestic bliss. Page after page of luscious items like: sock drawer dividers, microfibre dusters, recycling boxes, his and hers bucket buddies 'for those days when you both decide to spend the day weeding in the garden', microwave fresheners, wellington tidies and everything to make your life more ordered, more neat, more clean and more like Martha Stewart's. Why stop indoors? The garden is subject to Lakeland envy too: an irresistible garden camouflage range, to camouflage your garden furniture or dustbin or lawnmower. Because your garden should be neat and tidy too! Before you know where you are you would be popping one on anyone who sat still for longer than half an hour . . . Or asking your GRUMPY OLD MAN to wear one permanently. In fact why stop at making him wear it in the garden?

You are addicted, destined for a life of catalogues in the foreseeable future, on the slippery slope that leads to a personalised doormat or a bird table tidy, and you can do nothing about it, your days are now well and truly clogged up with it all. You're either ordering, receiving, picking up from the post office because you were out when the van came, querying your order in the telephone queue, or taking it back to the post office and standing in the queue. Your life is now catalogue led.

Once the companies all start to syndicate postcodes and names you are sunk – the postman has so many catalogues for you, he has to make a special trip to your house full of beige easy-care fabrics, with elasticated waists and apricot tops with appliquéd puppies or horses and an orgy of slip-on shoes, slip-on trousers, slip-on slips and tops that drop from the bust, which means you are officially dressed to run a bring-and-buy sale, not for getting off with anyone. You're doomed.

My mother – being that bit ahead of me in the age stakes and having had a Freeman catalogue habit most of her life – now has dozens of catalogue return packs by her front door at any one time. She is cheerfully spending my inheritance to boot.

TO DO
Send back boot tidy
Check VISA statesment for refund
                    from Lakeland

Take shoes
to repairer's

October 15th

The food allergist writes to me with her official findings
having done her scientific(!) analysis on my hair and lists what I
should and shouldn't eat from now on. Apparently the
scientific(!) tests show that I am allergic to both wheat and
dairy, which is going to make my life a bit tricky to say the least.
So now I am into specialist breads and milk – I need to buy
something called spelt flour bread, wheat-free pasta, goat's milk
or cheese, and soya milk. Yum. No wonder everyone loses weight.

TO DO
Go on internet for recipe for dairy
          and wheat-free Christmas cake.
Find cake-making woman to do birthday
               cake for YOUNGEST

Buy Granny
Trolley for
carrying loaves

October 16th

After driving 40 minutes out of my way on the way to work I find the specialist shop with spelt bread loaves. I stock up and buy four of the loaves, three to freeze and one to eat now. They are each of them heavier than house bricks, heavy enough to actually put your back out.

I might sue her.

October 17th

YOUNGEST announces at 9.45pm – just as she is going to bed – that she is making a swiss roll in domestic science, sorry I should say food technology, tomorrow. She needs all the ingredients weighed out and bagged up and in the basket for tomorrow morning otherwise Miss will be furious. Strikes me that weighing it all out is part of Miss's job description not mine, but she knows as well as I do that teenagers don't do anything as fiddly and time- consuming as that – and so she knows full well that their mothers will do it for them. I don't know why they can't weigh the wretched stuff out at school. But no, it's all designed to make our lives, my life, more difficult and more stressful, and make everyone else's easier and run smoother. Hence I hit Tesco's at 9.45pm, which is just when I really want to be sitting down, or lolling with a glass of wine, but now I'm here I might as well do the weekend shop despite the fact that I am in bad-tempered, horrible, spitty-type mood, because joy of joys, it will save me going tomorrow . . . In other words I shall be able to cross something off tomorrow's list which is officially fantastic.

I do the weekend shop and the domestic shop in record time, skim my trolley round the top of the aisles, taking the corners off, skidding up to raisins and baking and then back over to eggs and smoked salmon. It is blissfully empty, and since I know my way around the place so tragically well, I actually think I might do all my shopping on Thursdays at this time from now on. Yes, this is fantastic! Get to the counter and realise I have left my credit card at home because I left in such a huffy bad-tempered rush, and so only have £5 cash; once we have got it all halfway through the till, stupid gormless assistant has to get the supervisor over and they say they are about to close, and in the end I have to put everything else back other than for swiss roll recipe but come away with everything but the raisins. Have to call three of YOUNGEST friends' mothers to check if they can bring in enough raisins for us too. Two of them know nothing about the lesson and say that their darling must have already packed it all up. Model daughters evidently. It all takes until 10.30pm. To top it all Clarissa's mother (who does have spare raisins) takes the opportunity to rope me in for the Christmas Fayre at school running the bric-a-brac, which is code for a load of old junk no one wants that will need to be labelled up and lugged in and out of school and eventually just taken down to Oxfam. If I didn't have a life I would write in to the Head and complain.

To DO
Weekend shop

October 20th

What is it with compost heaps? Everyone else manages to get theirs to mulch down into black soil, like proper bought bagged-up compost, and mine just remains a big pile of leaves and potato peelings and weeds that smells in the corner of the garden and annoys me. It doesn't seem to decompose at all, just is basically an extension of the dustbins but smellier. Ring my mother and ask her advice – since she does gardening – and she says you have to turn it all over every few weeks, get a big fork at it and turn the whole thing over; also putting tea leaves on is supposed to help. Suddenly having a compost heap is another task, another job. I thought gardening was for retired people or was supposed to be relaxing. I think I shall go back to just binning it all up in bin bags with some household rubbish to fool the dustbin men again.

TO DO
Empty compost heap and take
                          it all to the tip
Buy more bin liners
Take leftover swiss roll to my mother's

October 31st

Hallowe'en. What a stupid idea that is. The shops are full of Hallowe'en merchandise. Even the local baker has got some Hallowe'en spider-topped cakes and orange and black biscuits. John Lewis has a full-on display of Hallowe'en-themed servicttes, hats and recipes mostly involving pumpkins. Sainsbury's staff are all dressed up in orange and black capes and horns, and suddenly Hallowe'en seems to have taken hold, like a bad computer virus. The shops are selling actual pumpkins, things the size of a lawnmower and as heavy that presumably we are all supposed to lug home, haul on to the kitchen work surface, peel, somehow, hollow out and make a spooky thing you put candles in, and then with all the hollowed-out flesh we are supposed to make more pumpkin pie, soup and stew than most families would eat in the whole year. It's just so stupidly American, and so obviously a way of getting us to spend more money. We British have Bonfire Night. We like Bonfire Night, it's nice and simple with bangers and baked potatoes and some sparklers and some fresh air and the smell of gunpowder, so why do we always have to copy the Americans?

YOUNGEST naturally watches so much American telly on Sky that she is much more into Hallowe'en than Bonfire Night, and her mates want to do trick or treat. I don't get trick or treat nor do I want to get it. I don't want my children going round to the local white trash knocking on their doors and running away, and I don't want them to come back with a load of old pick and mix that someone else has had their filthy hands on.

All this and having to eat five pieces of fruit and veg a day.

To Do
Tell GOM he has to forbid YOUNGEST
    doing trick or treat next year.
Why am I the only one to nag her?
Throw away some HARIBO sweets
    she got trick or treating
Remind GOM — has he got the DVD
        of RAT RACE yet?

November

November 1st

This year I am going to make Christmas really magical. ELDEST will be coming home, and our family will be complete once more. For once I shall make my own cake, pudding and mince pies. I might make my own mince meat too, how hard can it be? I browse through the Delia Christmas book and look at her luscious photos. Perhaps I should also crystallise some fruit, or preserve some plums in Kilner jars with tartan bows on? They'd make lovely presents for neighbours and aunts, and Mother-in-law would think I was a model wife.

November 3rd

On the train to London I am in same section as annoying man on mobile who has incredibly long conversation with his wife. When I say a long conversation I mean it goes on for a good 40 minutes. Naturally everyone in the carriage is treated to being

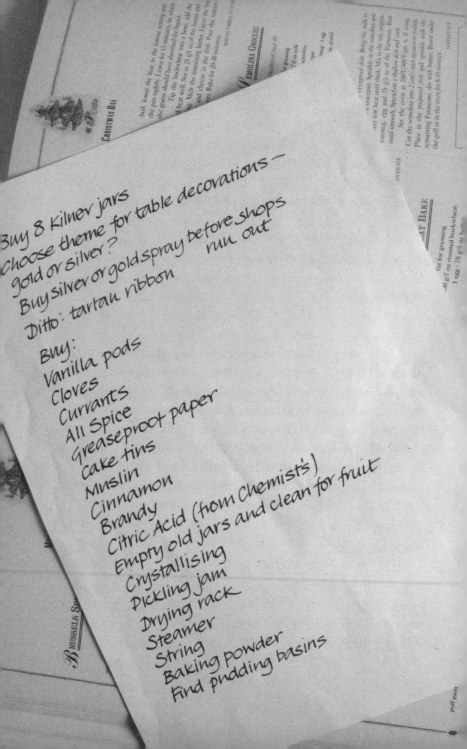

Buy 8 Kilner jars

Choose theme for table decorations —

gold or silver?

Buy silver or gold spray before shops run out

Ditto: tartan ribbon

Buy:
Vanilla pods
Cloves
Currants
All Spice
Greaseproof paper
Cake tins
Muslin
Cinnamon
Brandy
Citric Acid (from Chemist's)
Empty old jars and clean for fruit
Crystallising
Pickling jam
Drying rack
Steamer
String
Baking powder
Find pudding basins

able to hear every word – like any of us are in the least bit interested – on and on he drones . . . despite all my frowning and tutting and staring, he is oblivious. For a man of his age, and considering he is talking to his wife, the conversation is surprisingly racy; he's holding the phone like he's snogging it, he giggles, gets really animated. I am impressed, if I'm honest I'm a little bit jealous.

Conversations with GOM are by contrast rather matter of fact. Like 'Will you leave the milkman some money?', 'I'm on the one that gets in at 5.30', or 'Have you remembered to put the dustbin out because it's Thursday?' But by contrast, this is remarkably intimate. As in 'Are you still in bed, darling, how are the girls, what are you wearing to work today?', 'Are they still being horrid to you, my kitten?' I am irritated beyond measure a) because I'm a busy woman and have got a stack of things to do on my laptop and am finding it hard to concentrate, and b) because the gist of it is so in your face and oh how wonderful my marriage is. So I go up a gear and do a lot of huffing and puffing, slapping my book on the table and looking fed up. Not that he notices one bit.

We hear all about the business dinner he had last night, whom he was sat next to and that he got 'nicely merry'. Then, curiously, he asks her if there is any news on selling her house. Odd. At last he does the stupid love you love you thing as he hangs up. Good. But then, would you credit it – oh my God – he picks up the phone again almost immediately. So much for my huffing and puffing to shame him – I will have to go and get the guard and make huge fuss, but this time he gets an answer machine. 'Hi darling. Just to remind you I'm on the way back to London today. Must fix up something for our anniversary. Love you.' I think my mouth dropped open. So the first call was not to wife at all, but to lover, and this one is the poor wife unaware of the situation. If I was a real urban vigilante I would intervene. Do something. Make a citizen's arrest. Snatch his phone and dial his wife and tell her. Poor woman. No idea at all. I hate his silly little finger signature ring and posh accent. Probably so does his wife. She'll be well shot of him. Things are never what they seem.

To Do
Write to GNER about mobile use
         on trains (ask for fare reduction)
Kilner jars

November 4th

YOUNGEST's birthday. There is no big sister as big sister has flown the nest, but we do what we always do and put balloons down the staircase and the big Happy Birthday poster in the kitchen and the presents on the sofa, but it's not quite the same without her big sister. GOM triumphantly presents her with *The Rat Race* DVD. At least he's managed that! She opens it and looks dismayed . . . 'What's *Rat Pack*?' she says. 'I asked for *Rat Race* not *Rat Pack*. And anyway who are Dean Martin and Frank Sinatra?' Honestly, you'd think that some alarm bells would have gone off. Why on earth would a fourteen-year-old want a DVD with Dean Martin? Dur. Usual story, if you want something doing, do it yourself.

To Do
Take back RAT RACE DVD
        to Woolworth

November 5th

I decide to make Bonfire Night extra special, to show YOUNGEST how much better it is than stupid Hallowe'en. I throw a bit of a party with some of the neighbours and old friends, tell her she can ask as many friends as she likes and organise some games. In short, I try to recreate my own childhood Bonfire Night parties. I couldn't find a toffee apple recipe, so had to ring my mother (got involved in who is going where at Christmas conversation – always tricky). She had lost hers but says it is dead easy. You put about two bags of sugar to a quarter of a pint of water, cook it till it bubbles for about half an hour and then dip your apples in. Easy. Let them dry on racks and marvellous fun had by all.

Spend most of my lunch hour finding stick things to put apples on, none of the shops sell them, but have plenty of Hallowe'en trash still on knock-down offer, so I have to buy thin barbecue spikes and cut them in half, then rope them together like a little splint to hold the weight. All maddeningly time-consuming, but they are going to be very good indeed. Might make enough for next day as well as I imagine they are going to be very popular. Put in four bags of sugar and double the water and leave to heat up very hot on a high jet while I busy myself with baked potatoes, sausages, toad in the hole and organising the apple-bobbing bucket.

Clarissa rings about the bric-a-brac stall and her silly wretched Christmas Fayre, and has a long list of things I need to do, and some dates for my diary (has she got nothing else to do?) but have to break off when the smoke alarms go off, and rush into the kitchen full of thick dark black smoke like the ones they show you in those scary public health films telling you that Smoke Can Kill . . . which having witnessed some of it at first hand I can now believe. Open all the windows, manage to get pan outside the back door still bubbling and smoking like a volcano and begin cleaning up the mess. Takes me a good 30 minutes to clear the smoke, deactivate the smoke alarms and see the full scale of the damage. Bubbling 'toffee' has boiled all over the cooker hob and dripped down front of cooker itself, a trail of solidified toffee indicates exact path of burning pan's exit, and then outside on back doorstep the thing is still smouldering, still steaming and hissing like a pressure cooker. Imagine singe mark on step will be something that remains for several generations.

The remaining hour before guests arrive is spent whizzing round the kitchen making up for lost time with rest of cooking and party prep. GOM comes home with dismal selection of fireworks. I accuse him of leaving it as usual to the last minute but he says he had major trouble even finding a newsagent's that sells them. YOUNGEST and her friends were ever so slightly interested in my indoor sparklers and cascading fountain. I had a lovely time standing at the window looking at fireworks going off in other people's gardens and standing at the back door taking in the smell of it all. I bore the kids rigid with my memories of Bonfire Nights. YOUNGEST looks at me pityingly. I'm on my way to being so old I like coach trips, a run out or a walk around the garden centre. On my way to being so old people applaud me for knowing my own age.

To DO

Find receipt for RAT PACK DVD
New smoke alarms
Call Clarissa and say the toffee apples
   not a good idea for Christmas
           Fayre after all

November 6th

What is it with cleaners? You pay them to clean your house
and then they fail to clean it PROPERLY. How many times have I
asked her to do the bathroom mirror with the glass cleaner
product, and to please remember to put Hoover back in
cupboard under the stairs. Over the years I have written endless
nice notes with kisses at the end saying, would she mind awfully
or sorry to be so picky but could she possibly remember   if she
has time – to clean the bathroom mirror etc. etc., then I come
back home and nine times out of ten – guess what – the Hoover
is still in hall, and bathroom mirror spattered!!!! I am getting to
the stage where I intentionally put a mark on the bathroom
mirror on a Friday morning and rush upstairs when I come
home from work to check whether it's gone. For some reason it's
impossible to talk to cleaners like you talk to anyone else,
impossible to say 'look, when you clean the house you must do
the bathroom mirror please'. There should be a contract with a
clause in it, as in a job description, that way no one could
quibble with it. I want to say 'look here, lady, pull your socks up
or you're out', But no, I pussyfoot around the problem, which
kind of makes it worse.

More wiry hairs have appeared under my nose, a couple of them poking out of my nose. I am turning into GOM with grey hair and a beard, and he is turning into me with big bum and the start of boobs. The tweezers have become all-important daily weapon against this tendency of mine to turn into a man. Tweezing them out is murder and hurts like hell. I complain about YOUNGEST spending all her time in the bathroom but am frankly nearly as bad. Stare at myself in the bathroom mirror for a good five minutes. The double chin is horrendous. Wish I could do a Jeremy Beadle and grow one of those silly trompe l'oeil beards that go round your jawline, don't amount to much but trick the eye and disguise your three chins. Actually looking at the growth under my chin I could get lucky. It's simply so much easier for men, to lose their looks, get fat and old and hairy and bald simultaneously. For us it is really and truly hard.

To DO
Write note to Joan about Hoover
      being left out and bathroom mirror
Beauticians :
Bikini wax
Leg wax
Chin wax

November 8th

Christmas is simply not going to go away. They have been playing the Slade 'Do You Know It's Christmas' in Boots and Safeway's for weeks, everyone is in Operation Christmas mode. There are some people at work who have already done their shopping! Done it! Only got to wrap it up. Other people pretend they haven't done anything but they have, like students who pretend they have not done any revision for the exam when in fact they've been revising for weeks, so have all the women at work. I've seen the carriers by their desks. They have so started. I have not. Because the moment I start is the moment I get a whole new 'to do' list, the one that is the biggest of the year. The one that dwarfs all other 'to do' lists. But try as I might to ignore it, I am going to have to face it. It is going to be my life sentence for the next seven weeks, and is going to cost me an obscene amount of money. I am doomed.

To DO
Find receipt for RAT PACK DVD
Buy Christmas edition of PRIMA

November 12th

Another funeral. Inevitably the older you are, the more funerals there are to go to; I guess once you are in your seventies they become one of your main social activities, meeting up with your ever decreasing circle of mates. It's a nice day out – unless of course you were incredibly close to the newly dead, in which case it is somewhat different, but with a neighbour or a distant uncle it's a celebration, a party with real camaraderie, some sandwiches and some uplifting thoughts. I like the speeches, the dedications, the lovely things people say about their friends and family, the feeling of getting a good sob out of your system. I like a nice rousing hymn like 'Abide with Me' or 'Jerusalem'. It's good for the soul. Today's was a Quaker funeral which, if you can have a favourite sort, is mine. Think I might go for a Quaker funeral myself . . . then again not sure. Big decision. Love the way everyone who wants to can stand up and say what they want, dedicate a poem, retell an anecdote, say what they will always remember of the person. Lovely way to do it.

We stream out of the church into the winter sunshine, and go to Mary's for some vol-au-vents and a glass of sherry, with some Van Morrison playing as that was his favourite music.
A lovely day.

TO DO
Find out if you can have a Quaker
    funeral if you're not a Quaker
Suggest GOM talks to close friends
    and subtly warns them that I would
    like some poems and a Quaker funeral;
that way when the time comes they
    might have things prepared
Marinate fruit for cake
Buy fruit for preserving

November 13th

Write polite but firm note to Joan saying she must remember to do the bathroom mirror. I still put a please on the end and a kiss, but spend the whole day at work wondering whether when I come home she will have turned over a new leaf with my newfound courage and direct approach and realise who's boss.

Have to call YOUNGEST to say not to use the bathroom until I get home, that it must be just as Joan left it, it is a virtual crime scene. If they sold that red and white stripy tape at Tesco's, I would have bought some, rope it off like they do in those murder programmes. YOUNGEST's phone not on – naturally – so have to text her which takes me ages since it is so complicated. She texts back after school with just a ? mark, so I have to leave her a long message on the answer machine and text her again to make sure she listens to answer machine before she goes upstairs to bathroom.

I drive home with a sense of real urgency, like a detective approaching the scene of crime. I race upstairs two at a time, keys still swinging in the door, and put the bathroom light on for a really good look. Streaks and splatters that I left there this morning while setting the trap. She has not done the mirror. Temper boiling, rage setting in, I stomp down the landing and open the cupboard under the stairs and no Hoover, she has left the Hoover in spare room still plugged in. Still plugged in! She has never done that before! My bossy tone has backfired and now I am sunk. I shall have to either give in and she will have the upper hand for ever more, or find another cleaner, and that – I know – is going to take me months. Skid up to notepad by phone to see whether she perhaps hasn't read the note. Maybe we can still be friends. Or pretend to be. But oh yes, she has read my note all right. Next to my note she has written her own note. She says she has run out of Windolene spray so that's why she hasn't done the mirror. She has so not run out of Windolene. I swear there was one at least half full. She has probably thrown it away. Get my rubber gloves on and consider going through bins to check whether she chucked it out, but of course I realise I could go through all the week's rubbish and even if I found the Windolene among all the chicken drumsticks and week's kitchen rubbish she might have been clever enough to empty it first so that, when I did find it, it would serve me right for being such a difficult cow. It would be a job for forensic.

There is no way I am going to win. She knows that.

TO DO

Put note up in Co-op for cleaner on index card thing, with my mother's number on it in case Joan reads it and recognises my number

Ask around at work for cleaners

November 14th

Get invited to a dinner party and unavoidably have to accept. I am going to have to make polite conversation for a tryingly long time. Get there and the two other couples look very middle-aged, look, frankly, a bit dull, and the shocking truth is that you've been invited with them because presumably your hosts thought you would have a lot in common which is code for they think you're a bit dull too. Hostess says they have just come back from South Africa – resist sounding too interested lest they get the snaps out – but not content with telling us that they went to South Africa and had a lovely time, they treat us to the full route, towns, names, dates and historical points of interest. And there doesn't seem to be anything remotely like cooking going on in the kitchen.

Eventually hostess says she had better put the meat in. Meat 'in', that means in the oven presumably. Meat 'on' might be more encouraging as in she just has to fry it or boil it, but meat 'in' implies that the bloody meal hasn't even been started. Clearly the whole thing is going to take hours and hours . . . You start to do a time estimate, three courses and then coffee, that's got to be two hours at least, once the food is cooked. I go to the loo and really take my time, don't even need the loo, put some make-up on, steal some moisturiser, fiddle about looking in their bathroom cabinet – anything to kill time. Come down and they're still talking about their second homes or some dreary conversation about decking their garden or something. If only I could go back up to the bathroom and run myself a bath. Perhaps I should encourage everyone who knows me to think that my old age is going to be very eccentric indeed and they will take such behaviour in their stride.

BUY SOME CHOCOLATES FOR JOAN

November 15th

I am getting so jumpy. I mean obviously I am jumpy when the cat brings something in, or a bird comes in the living room, but I am getting so jumpy I do that silly middle-aged-woman little scream when someone walks into the room unexpectedly, or the other day when the toast popped up. It's what my mother would have called 'trouble with her nerves'.

TO DO
Sort out photos into albums
Buy homeopathic Rescue Remedy

November 17th

Bought myself a mac. An off-white Burberry sort of job. Nothing fancy, but thought it would go with everything, the sort of non fashion statement someone of my age should go in for. Bumped into my mother in town and realised it was virtually identical to hers.

TO DO
Find bag for mac and receipt to take
        back TOMORROW
Sort out holiday photos
Call Co-op to check if anyone has
        left number for cleaning job with them

November 21st

Write nice newsy jolly note to Joan next to box of chocolates saying I know how busy she must be with the run-up to Christmas, so if she doesn't have time to do everything I understand. She leaves me a note back saying she will be leaving at the end of the week. No explanation. This is my punishment obviously for using the word 'Must' in my note last week. Serves me right. Now I will have to deal with the run-up to Christmas without any help around the house.

TO DO
Make rota for family to help
                            clean honse

Show GOM how to use Hoover
                            attachments

November 23rd

Clarissa calls stupid meeting after school pick up about Christmas Fayre. Like that was supposed to be convenient for me! Which it would be if I was a stay-at-home mum like she is. You might know it clashed with meeting Jocasta called, so had to say I had been called out to see a client. Left it vague, said they could get me on the mobile.

Clarissa has typed out an agenda, had her hair done, and has set herself a table at the front of the room like she's top dog. Honestly, haven't these women got better things to do? The headmistress comes in and greets Clarissa with grovelling gratitude, and says she has popped her head round the door to thank Clarissa for all her tremendous hard work once more this year and knows that with Clarissa at the helm the thing will go with a zing as usual. It all becomes crystal clear. Clarissa troubles herself with all this, not because she has nothing to do, but because she is parent-in-chief, top of headmistress's good books. If she wants daughter to move French sets, or get a place in the badminton club or trampolining at lunchtime club, all she has to do is snap her little manicured fingers. Because Clarissa is in charge of all the tedious fund-raising activities in the school calendar.

Other trainee Clarissas speak up nicely when spoken to by her, when asked how their cake stall is going, or the prizes for the raffle, or the wickerwork stall or the organic Christmas Fayre stall. Masterfully she has got an army of other women on the case, ringing round local beauticians and Italian restaurants, grovelling for sponsorship and raffle prizes and suchlike. This woman should be running a multinational.

She gets to me as the new girl and asks how I am getting on with bric-a-brac, do I have a theme? What sort of stall was I thinking of? The question took me by surprise, what I want to say is, 'Well I imagine I just sort of bung on a trestle table a load of crap that gets sent in because nobody wants it or can flog it on eBay and I lay it all out and if I have time I price it all with little sticky labels, otherwise I have a coffee and wait for people to ask, then at the end I take the unsold stuff, which will be most of it, and stick it on Oxfam's step where they tell you not to on a Saturday night but everybody does anyway.'

'A theme? How do you mean?'

'Well, last year bric-a-brac took a record £300, it was a Victorian theme, year 9 tied it in with a history project and Miss Jones (headmistress) got very involved.' What she is doing is throwing me a rope of opportunity to be in Miss Jones's good books. 'Oh I see. Hadn't really thought about it.' 'Can I suggest that you email me some thoughts by end of play Friday?' She's worse than Jocasta. Scary woman, obviously must have been head girl in her day.

The meeting carries on for 1 hour and 40 minutes more with details of where in the assembly hall each stall will be, who is doing mince pies and teas and coffees, pricing decisions, lucky dips, entry charges, raffle tickets, helium balloons and ads in local paper. Sneak out when Clarissa busy with caretaker and cleaning arrangements and she shouts as I try and sneak out, 'Shall I put you down for hall clearing afterwards?' There is no sneaking out when Clarissa is about.

This is all I need in the run-up to Christmas.

December

December 1st

Christmas task frenzy is getting into full gear, am completely bogged down with tasks. Saw someone reading *The Little Book of Calm* on my way in to work. Felt like snatching it and flapping it over their head. Childish thought.

To Do
Send letter out to parents about
      bric-a-brac needed
Christmas cake ingredients —URGENT
Buy Christmas cards
Second-class stamps
Preserve fruit and put in kilner jars

December 2nd

I can put it off no longer, the Christmas 'to do' lists have to be written out. Unlike my daily 'to do' lists, this is the list to end all lists. It is going to be so big it might require a clipboard to hold it all together. My mother has given me her list covering a sheet of A4 of things she needs me to buy for her to give to other people, as has my mother-in-law. Both claim that they can't cope with the Christmas crowds and that their legs are bad . . . And that they would only get it wrong if they chose the presents themselves and everything would only have to go back. And I certainly don't want their 'taking back' lists, that's for sure. Their legs are bad . . . neat excuse . . . So now I have three lists on the go: my own and theirs. The list – as in the master list, the amalgamation of the lists – goes something like this: presents for my mother-in-law to give my children, presents for my mother-in-law to give to her son, presents from my mother to give to me, presents for my mother to give to her sister in Australia . . . On and on and on they go . . . I fantasise about getting them both into one of those nice new retirement homes on the main road next to the busy bus lane – with luck I might go down to just the one extra list next year. Wicked thought. The Christmas card ritual has to be started. Already they are coming in on a daily basis, some of them from people I literally do not remember at all. This year I am definitely going to streamline the list and I am going to do one of those computerised label things which means that I can print them all out on neat labels every year rather than go through the misery of writing them all

TO DO

Look in present-recycling cupboard
          and allocate some
Buy posh wrapping paper for
                    recycled presents
Preserve fruit and put in kilner jars
Pyjamas for Christmas Eve

PRESENTS TO DO LIST

Mothers presents to:

ME - pink leather gloves, wine glasses

GOM - jazzy tie, leather slippers

ELDEST - new Madonna CD
iPod charger thingy

YOUNGEST - sparkly silver top SIMMS
Version 6

PRESENTS TO MY MOTHER

from me - National Trust Diary
new flask, oil paints

from GOM - beige polo neck
(Marks Classic range size

from ELDEST — ?

from YOUNGEST - posh soap.

PRESENTS from GOM to:

his Pa - Moulton Brown bath thingys

his mother - new Delia
Alan Bennett diary

Uncle Jack - tie and socks to match

his sister - coffee machine maker
thing (must do
cappuccinos

nephew - TOKENS

neice - TOKENS

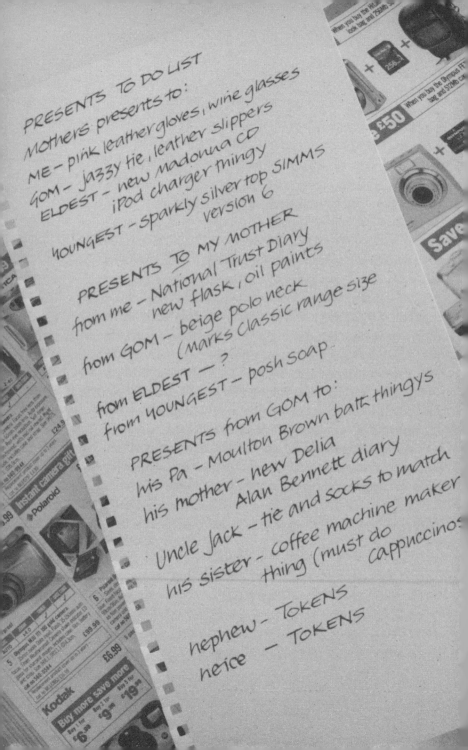

PRESENTS FROM ME to:

Office Secret Santa
GOM - gardening book, diary
ELDEST - Digital camera
         (ask her which make)
YOUNGEST - Hair straighteners
         must be ceramic

STOCKING FILLERS
Stocking main presents
Presents am
Presents pm
Presents for the dog
Presents from the dog
Pyjamas for Christmas Eve
Table presents
Nuts
Chocolate coins for Santa's trail
School secret Santa (13 year old)
Form teacher - soap
Next door - Celebrations box

out by hand. Enlist YOUNGEST to help me, and she is only half concentrating since she has a lot of urgent MSN messaging and lolling on her bed to do. Says it is as easy as anything. Gets me on to the right grid thing and so I devote the next three and a half hours typing out in maddeningly small boxes the names and addresses of all our Christmas card recipients.

Clarissa calls in the middle of it asking for an update. Like it's a massive work project not a stupid bric-a-brac stall, and I say I am waiting for the school secretary to send out my note round the school, which is not strictly true since I still haven't given it in yet. 'Strange,' she says, 'I talked to Margaret only today and she said she was still waiting for you to hand it in to her.' Nothing gets past Clarissa. Not a little white lie, not a little fib, nothing. I agree sheepishly to do it by tomorrow morning, but continue the labels task until 11.30pm, absolutely bushed. Tear up all the names and addresses, some of which were handwritten out ten years ago. Feel exhausted but that have made big progress.

TO DO

Buy Christmas cake (might distress it round the edges and pretend to mother-in-law I made it)
   —put own icing on

BRIC-A-BRAC round robin to school secretary

Buy sticky labels for computerised addresses

Take Kilner jars back and get money back

December 3rd

Write some Christmas cards at work while no one looking. Jocasta away at some daft conference. Marvellous feeling. Have to do a bit of cheating here and there as in 'Dear Roger and family', which is code for I have no idea what your wife and children are called but you seem to remember mine. It's all a total farce, but this year I am ahead of the game, hurrah, will manage to send them all Second class mail too. Even better.

Manage a long soak in the bath, light some of those candles people give you who have no idea what else to buy and are likely candidates for recycling. Begin to see the point of them. Lovely hot bath, lots of bubbles, might do this more often. Empty nests have their upsides.

My mother rings with a sob story about Derek and how she is dreading Christmas without my father. Well, here's a surprise. I'm dreading it too. But suddenly I'm the one that is supposed to do the mothering not her. Marvellous.

To DO
Grout mould off tiles by bath and
    get streaks off tiles
Buy 67 second-class Christmas stamps
Look out some crap from loft
            for bric-a-brac

December 4th

Not only are the present lists well under way, the food lists now have to come to the fore, because for some reason making one meal on Christmas Day with enough leftovers in the fridge to scavenge on until the supermarkets open again is a big deal. A big enough deal to send the entire female population into a food frenzy. And although I can rationalise that, can logically realise how silly it is to get sucked into all the panic, I do it again, like every year. This year both daughters have become veggies . . . So we have two vegetarian daughters, neither of whom likes vegetables – joy of joys – so try as I might to find something in Delia for them for Christmas Day, most of the

Veggie
food for
Christmas?
Quorn?
Fish fingers?

recipes – guess what – involve vegetables, or lentils which both of them detest along with all other pulses. At this rate I can see me giving them a fish finger or a Quorn burger each while we feast on a fatted goose. Literally. They don't even like nut cutlets.

Once the food tasks appear on the radar my whole life is cluttered up with it all – there are notes, lists, reminders now in my office, handbags, car and kitchen calendar is by now almost falling apart, the metal thing that holds it together at the top has come half out and so the pages don't fold over and the whole of December is a mess. Aunts, uncles, in-laws, school plays, parent charity nights, office parties, and then the Christmas period itself is getting horribly full with old friends', relatives' and neighbours' dos. It's not that I don't like them. OK most of them. It's just that every year I say to myself I am going to chill over Christmas instead of it being a race against time without a minute to even read the *Radio Times* or relax with a box of chocolate brazil nuts. That sort of thing would be my idea of Christmas . . . Some nice uninterrupted lolling on my own sofa in other words.

CALL AUNTY DOREEN – Is she coming for Boxing Day?

December 8th

Finally get YOUNGEST to help me back on silly computer grid with addresses on to print out darling white labels. She fiddles about with the cursor and asks me for the labels and I hand her the roll of labels bought from Smith's; she says they're the wrong sort, they have to be on A4 sheets not on a roll like the one I bought. How else do I think they are going to get through the printer, it's not a typewriter or something out of the ark, stupid. Dur.

To Do
Buy more sticky labels on A4 size
Buy extra cards for emergency bouncers
for people who send to me whom
I haven't sent to, plus take a pack
into the office

December 10th

Completely exhausted. Not only have I got more to do than last year, I realise that I simply don't have the energy I used to have. I used to be able to get up at 7am, prepare four packed lunches, put a wash on, do the ironing, go for an early morning swim, do a day's work, come home, cook tea, wash up, do some more ironing and an hour of personal admin or work at the computer, finish at 9.45 and find time to lay the table for breakfast. Now I am so rung out at the end of the day I could use a stairlift to get up the stairs to bed at night. It wouldn't be so bad if I managed to sleep through like the rest of the family do – I can't remember the last time I went to bed and slept till 7am. I am forever lying awake in a hot sweat, lying awake worrying about stuff that is in reality so trivial it is pitifully silly to worry about it at all, or am up and down to the loo two or three times in the night. I thought you were supposed to need less sleep as you got older, not true in my case, it's God's way of telling me that I have to slow down, but sadly there seems to be no sign of me being able to. It's His way of getting me used to the idea that some day relatively soon I'll be retired. Then I'll be up at 6.15 listening to Radio 4, or on a bad day *Farming Today*, have a

potter in the dressing gown, including some
gardening, lunch with a friend, have an
afternoon nap, eat tea at 7pm with *The
Archers*, and climb into bed at 9.30. It'll be
like being back at nursery again.
Eventually even the nappies will be
back. Bring it on I say.

FINISH
ENVELOPE
LABELS !!
URGENT !!

TO DO
Call Clarissa
Go to computer shop for special
                    address labels

December 12th

Get YOUNGEST back on the computer with new labels. She
whizzes about with the cursor again and says OK now it should
work. Presses something and it all whizzes into action. Walk out
of room while it is printing to look at the sum total of the bric-a-
brac offered so far from school and what I have managed to get
from the loft. It amounts to two boxes of cracked crockery, a
nasty bright pink vase, a broken Toby jug, a biscuit tin with a
dodgy lid and some unwanted presents that have been doing the
rounds for long enough that they now couldn't go in the
Tombola but might pass here for bric-a-brac. Everyone has been
watching too many *Flog It* programmes or *Antique Roadshows*.
Anything of value at all that is kicking around in the house has
either been taken to a car boot sale or been sold on eBay. Shall
have to go to all the charity shops in town to gather up a

respectable amount and then suggest to Clarissa that I just perch with assembled crap on the end of Tombola, as a sort of added bonus, come afterthought. I could call it a postscript as it sounds posher.

Back upstairs to stick labels on envelopes that I have already put stamps on. Excited! Get up there and they are all on the floor printed out and feel truly satisfied. Get the first one out to peel off and to my horror they have printed, but each address has printed just that little bit too far down the label and so each address straddles two labels which means that to use them you have to peel two off, and then cut them in half. Which considering there are 65 of them is going to take me a good two hours more since every time you cut one in half it sticks to itself and you have to prise it open again, and then it doesn't stick down as well as it should and you have to put a bit of Pritt glue underneath one of the corners, and then you get the glue on your fingers and it takes some of the writing off the labels and you have to handwrite some of the letters back in. Get the picture?

I could have written them all out by hand by now and posted a week ago. Have to leave it for tomorrow and throw the labels in the corner of the room in a fit of childish temper. Was banking on having at least Christmas cards ticked off the list by now.

To DO
Call Clarissa
Finish card envelopes

December 13th

Had a brainwave.

Why not do the Christmas supermarket shop on line? Why wait until the whole world is shopping for brandy butter and sprouts? Do it now. Get something crossed off the list. Anything to avoid the scrum at the supermarket again at 06.20, the queue to pick up the ORDERED turkey (when there are hundreds on the shelves) and the fight over the last red cabbage. An hour into the process and I was feeling decidedly relieved. The colour was coming back to my cheeks. Organic turkey, sprouts, parsnips, smoked salmon, gravy granules (sorry to shock you) and fresh custard, all in my virtual trolley. If I was actually in the supermarket I would be skipping in the aisles, singing, probably singing, 'Happy Talk' from *South Pacific*. Even spent an extra 15 minutes stocking up on all the essentials that you inevitably run out of on Dec 27th – loo roll, washing-up liquid, washing powder, paper serviettes, spare batteries even – felt like I could really enjoy Christmas this year, could concentrate on wrapping presents beautifully and extending some nice good cheer and neighbourliness all around. I might get round to cleaning the car for Christmas, or dry-cleaning some cushions . . . Life is good.

I get to the virtual checkout. Fiddle about in the stupid address box when it says it is not the correct address and you know it is just because you have missed out a space or something. Horrific bill. Decide that delivery on Christmas Eve morning would be best – cutting it a bit fine I know but then at least you know it will all be done. Get to the page with delivery slots. To my horror all the ones AFTER DEC 10TH AND BEFORE JANUARY 1ST HAVE GONE! All allocated to women who are evidently more organised with more time on their hands than me. Like Clarissa for instance. Have to fish out shopping list from bin again, I could weep. Have wasted two and a half hours. Perhaps I should go to anger management courses, or maybe they should offer them free AT THE SUPERMARKET.

Call a non-virtual supermarket to see if they can offer any immediate task reduction, and try to order turkey, and they say you have to come in in person or do it on-line. Ring local butcher and leave message on answer machine. Job still not done. Nothing shifted off my 'to do' list, and now have wasted whole morning. Could sob.

To DO
Look into frozen turkeys
Finish card envelopes

December 14th

The Christmas Fayre. Needless to say my bric-a-brac offerings
were greeted with such disdain by Clarissa and her committee
that I might as well have been showing them the inside of the
dog poo bin in the park.

'I think we'd better draft you in on hair braiding. Sophie is
short of a pair of hands. And we shall need you to clear the hall
by 6pm, there's a barn dance in tonight.' Great.

A queue of 12 children all wanting their hair braided when
their parents have paid £2.50 for it is not a nice way to spend
your Saturday when you can't braid hair. Frowns and tuts all
round; one or two of the braids had unravelled before they even
got back to their parents to show them.

December 15th

The last but one Sunday before Christmas which means that
the whole world is shopping. Including me. I thought I had
almost finished but then both daughters have revised their
Christmas lists, which means not only do I still have long list of
presents still to buy, I have some taking back to do before I start.
Takes 45 minutes to find somewhere to park – 45 minutes! And
the parking space is just that bit too far to keep going back to fill
the boot. So I have to lug everything around with me like a
homeless bag lady but more bad-tempered. Prices at this stage
of the game are irrelevant, price comparisons just not realistic.
All you want to do is get things ticked off the list, you don't care
in what order, you don't care in what colour. Ticks are what you
want. Ticks are what you live for.

Every single thing you buy involves queuing, well OK so

maybe if you were buying bathing costumes or sun block you'd have a teeny bit of space, but on the whole if you're on soaps and calendars, everyone else is doing the same. You want Sims 6, so does everyone else, you want an iPod speaker, so does everyone else. Maddening, maddening, maddening.

GIVE - GOM the labels problem

December 16th

The office party. Obviously huge pointless crisis as to what to wear. After trying on at least six outfits, I plump for the ubiquitous floaty top with the camisole under showing a bit of cleavage which I notice is looking what ELDEST would call a bit dodgy, a bit wrinkly . . . Maybe I have reached the stage where my cleavage should not see the light of day. Party is predictably hideous. There's a lot of flirting, a lot of drinking, one or two of the girls in the office have hired sexy Santa outfits, which is maddening – showing a lot of leg and making me look even frumpier than I feel – and inevitably Robin and Jocasta get into a bit of a huddle. One of the marvellous things about getting older is that if you want to make your excuses and leave such a ghastly event at 8pm you can, not only is it allowed, it is positively welcomed by all the young people who are dying to get off with one another and don't want to waste time talking to you. I see Robin has got Jocasta pinned to the wall in deep conversation, and I decide to leave. Get the lift to find a sweet-looking bloke asking if I know

needs ironing

where he can find Jocasta. Must be her stay-at-home husband, she is a lucky girl that's for sure. See my opportunity and rather than telling him where the party is, I take him, show him, take no risks. Sometimes I can be such a cow.

GOM has he done me labels?

TO DO
Send creepy email to Jocasta's boss
    with some ideas for next year

December 17th

ELDEST comes home and her room instantly looks messed up again, which I find oddly thrilling. It is so wonderful to have her home I could skip, skip along the landing, and skip around the kitchen. Take her breakfast in bed, and get all excited about our imminent family Christmas. Who cares about all the chores and tasks, my family is under one roof and I have not a care in the world. The Christmas decorations go up. When the girls were little this was a magical process and it retains some of its magic for this reason. But this year there is tangibly less enthusiasm from the children, its me that's overexcited, me that puts the Christmas carols CD on, me that is trying to recreate a scene from *It's a Wonderful Life*.

GOM persuades the girls to go and buy the Christmas tree with him. I suspect it will be the last time ELDEST gets the tree with us, and it is outrageously large, it's a kind of male version of a hot flush – his way of trying to recreate their childhood too. He knows full well that ELDEST next year will have left home and getting her back in time to buy the tree will be impossible; she'll probably cut it so fine she'll be back on Christmas Eve itself. Once YOUNGEST leaves we'll be into artificial trees.

GOM still not done the Christmas card labels, so spend an infuriating hour cutting and sticking the last 20. Crawl into bed at 1.30am.

December 18th

TAKE CARDS
TO POST
OFFICE

Take the wretched cards into the post office and I have, joy of joys, just missed the second-class posting deadline, so I have to buy 67 x 8p stamps to make them up to the right postage and stand in the post office and stick them on all of the envelopes. Push them in the postbox with anger and resolve never to do Christmas cards again. But I think I said that last year too.

TO DO
Pick up frozen turkey
Buy Christmas pudding
and mince pies

December 21st

Major wrapping session. Sellotape can be really spiteful at this time of year. I tear off little bits and put them on my dressing table and gouge off chunks which takes chunks off the varnish. If you tear strips and put them on the carpet it just loses its stick, and on the kitchen table it doubles up on itself and knots into a ball. Then it runs out after about three presents. You thought you would wrap them all up in one horrible trying session, but the task spreads across two or three days. One way or the other, as fast as you are ticking things off your list, other things are going on instead. Nothing finishes. You are never done. Not until you have fallen over in a heap on Dec 24th at 11.30pm. Then you stop. You have to stop. The shops have closed. Can't they just be closed for the whole of December and then we might all be in with a chance of actually enjoying some of it?

December 23rd

Decide to delegate. Give GOM a carefully written shopping list for supermarket. For once he can experience the hell of it. Put it in aisle order, so that he hits the sprouts and red cabbage first and ends with dry ginger ale. It's all very detailed as if written for an alien, so when it says 'satsumas', it says 'satsumas NOT oranges', and next to 'tomatoes' it says NICE TOMATOES – PLEASE CHECK THEY ARE NOT SQUISHY, and next to 'double cream' it says CHECK SELL-BY DATE... It's taken me so long to write out the blooming list I might as well have gone myself.

6pm I text him to see how he is getting on with list. He texts back saying he is going after Christmas drinks at work. Cool as you like. I call him and say he has to go now lest they have run out of sprouts or stuffing or brandy butter. Now as in now, this minute. 9pm no sign of him. 9.30 I call him and he is in Tesco's, apparently he can't find fresh custard: 'Is it in a tin?' He has spent 15 minutes just looking for the custard: Why he doesn't just ask someone I have no idea. Honestly, you want something done do it yourself . . .

He comes home with it all at 10pm and there are a series of maddeningly not quite right disappointments, the stuffing is in a packet! For goodness sake! The custard is in a carton as in long life, and of course the satsumas have no green leaves on. Worse, he has made some shopping decisions of his own and bought the largest jar of pickled onions I have ever seen, so big it won't fit into the cupboard standing up but has to be screwed up tight and put in horizontally or has

to sit on the work surface until used up which at the rate we eat pickled onions will be well into the next decade. He says they were on offer. Yes, of course they were on offer, no one in their right mind wanted them.

To Do
Go back to supermarket for
fresh stuffing, satsumas
with leaves on and fresh custard
Buy pork pies to go with pickled onions

December 24th

Make mince pies with ready-to-roll pastry and jar of mince meat. OK, it wasn't exactly what Delia would have done, but it is something. I have my pinny on, ELDEST is at home, OK watching Sky Plus with her sister, the pantry is full, GOM is messing about trying to get the Christmas fairy lights to work (and failing) and my mother is doing the ironing. We're not having a riotous time, but I feel cautiously content for once. I have a feeling that as time goes by Christmas will in fact be the time I look forward to the most, the time when my daughters will feel obliged to come home with their boyfriends and then their own children. Or until they allow me to do some ironing for them while they are busy running around for their own families. Sneak behind the sofa while they are watching TV and kiss the top of both their heads. Once a mother always a mother.

TO DO
Sort out old family Christmas
    photos for Christmas Day
Soak dishcloth in bleach

MY CURRENT TOP GRUMPS

Muffins – what happened to cakes?

People spitting and weeing and sicking up on the pavement – someone is going to do themselves a nasty injury sliding on it.

Stickers on back of cars are getting silly . . . *Who cares who's on board* would be a better idea. Might invent them.

American speak – can we stop ticking boxes and thinking outside boxes and pushing envelopes? More silliness.

Why does everything have to have Aloe Vera in it? I don't need my loo paper to have it in – whatever it is or whoever Vera is.

Gravy granules.

Shoe shop assistants.

Panty liners with deodorant.

Teenage girls' magazines.

Linen I just look like I forgot to iron it.

People who constantly say 'love you love you' after phone calls.

Other people – trouble is if I'm in a car then I'm annoyed with the pedestrians and if I'm a pedestrian then I'm annoyed with the cars. Take the pedestrian crossing outside the main station in the city centre. If I'm driving past I get held up for about five minutes waiting for all the pedestrians to dribble over, pulling their wobbly trolleys, laden down with bags. I am annoyed at them. Then next day I might be walking over the same crossing on my way from the station to the office, and guess what, I feel like saying to the drivers, 'Look, it's blowing a gale here, actually I'm getting soaked waiting for you to stop for me to cross so look that's just not fair.'

And breathe.

THINGS THAT MAKE ME GRUMPY
ABOUT THE MAN I LIVE WITH

- Why doesn't he start by looking in the right place instead of shouting, *'It's not there'* or *'You've moved it,'* while turning house upside down. What does he want . . . a grid reference?

- Toilet rolls – presumably he thinks they grow on holders.

- There is a difference between the laundry basket and the floor.

- Dishes and cutlery – no they don't levitate to kitchen sink or dishwasher on their own.

- Just because it's Buy One Get One Free doesn't mean we want two of them or even one of them thank you.

- Stop buying huge family packs of cereals and coffee at the supermarket. Yes, it might be good value but they don't fit in the cupboard.

- Please will you throw away those corduroy shoes.

THINGS THAT CHEER US UP

- Our children
- Trees
- Sunshine
- Free parking
- Catalogues
- Cleaning the shower grouting with an old electric toothbrush head
- Finding any uses for old electric toothbrush head
- Using up leftovers
- Someone who knows about fish at the fish counter
- Parking in the parent and child bays in Tesco's. Well, I have my mother in the car – what's the difference?
- A bath

THINGS THAT MAKE US CRY

- *Bambi*
- Nativity plays
- *Peekaboo* books
- *Wonderful Life*
- The smell of our children's hair
- Our empty nests
- Our father's hankies

Acknowledgements

I would like to thank my lovely husband Michael Parker for being such a brilliant Grumpy Old Man both on and off screen, and for generally being able to retain his sense of humour and optimism when I lose both. This book would not have been possible without my mother, Jean Holder, since her support, encouragement and love have made me the person I am today, which is another way of saying I trained as a Grumpy Old Woman under her. I hope that my two gorgeous daughters Siena and Ellen will forgive me for writing a book that in places draws on our lives together, although I emphatically deny ever having tried to open one of their diaries. I thank them for just being them really, and hope that this insight into the mind of a middle-aged woman will mean that they approach their own midlife, when it eventually comes, with affectionate memories of our family life. I would like to also thank Suzanne Lee and Anne Leuchars for their creative input – a result of being both inventively funny and of a similar grumpy disposition.

The television series would not have happened in the first place without Stuart Prebble, whose judgement and creative support I have come to treasure and enjoy enormously. The brilliantly funny and original Grumpy Old Women on screen have been a huge source of inspiration, and I am indebted to all of them:

Aggie Mackenzie

Ann Widdecombe

Annette Crosbie

Arabella Weir

Dillie Keane

Esther Rantzen

Germaine Greer

Helen Lederer

Indira Joshi

Jane Moore

Jenni Trent Hughes

Jenny Eclair

Kathryn Flett   Muriel Gray
Kim Woodburn   Pam St Clement
Linda Robson   Sheila Hancock
Maureen Lipman   Stephanie Beacham
Michele Hanson

I would like to thank in particular Jenny Eclair whose humour, talent and support have been astonishingly important to me as a writer and as a woman who has really bad taste in shoes. I am her number one fan.

Thanks also to Alison Steadman for her brilliant reading of my scripts on screen, and whose wit and wisdom make the whole process enjoyable. From Liberty Bell Productions I would like in particular to thank Claire Storey Lambert who directed and edited the TV series, and whose judgement and creativity is scarily flawless, Fahima Chowdhury whose organisational skills are scarily wonderful, Steph Robinson and Emma McKinney who contributed enormously to the TV series and who are remarkably ungrumpy. Thanks to the BBC – to Elaine Bidell, Maxine Watson and Mirella Breda for believing in me and letting me have a ball while making some hopefully entertaining TV. Last but not least, thanks to the clever and gifted Lucinda McNeile, Alan Samson, Ruth Muray and George Sharp at Weidenfeld & Nicolson.